AN INQUIRY, &c.

Dublin: Printed by JOHN S. FOLDS, 5, Bachelor's Walk.

AN INQUIRY

INTO THE

PRINCIPAL POINTS OF DIFFERENCE,

REAL OR IMAGINARY,

BETWEEN THE TWO CHURCHES,

WITH A VIEW TO RELIGIOUS HARMONY OR FORBEARANCE.

TOGETHER WITH

SOME REMARKS RELATIVE TO THE PRESENT EXTRAORDINARY TIMES.

BY

THE REV. DAVID O'CROLY,

AUTHOR OF "THE ESSAY ON ECCLESIASTICAL FINANCE,"

ETC. ETC.

DUBLIN.

MILLIKEN AND SON, GRAFTON-STREET,

BOOKSELLERS TO THE UNIVERSITY.

LONDON: B. FELLOWES, LUDGATE-STREET.

1835.

But such is the lot of all that deal in public affairs, whether of church or commonwealth, that which men list to surmise of their doings, be it good or ill, they must, beforehand, arm their minds to endure. Wherefore to let go private surmises, whereby the thing in itself is not made either better or worse, if just and allowable reasons might lead them to do as they did, then are *these censures all frustrate.*—HOOKER, *Book* 4, *sect.* 14.

Thus the poor Hugonots of France were engaged in a civil war by the specious pretences of some who, under the guise of religion, sacrificed so many thousand lives to their own ambition and revenge. Thus was the whole body of Puritans in England drawn to be instruments or abettors of all manner of villainy by the artifices of a few men whose designs from the first were levelled to destroy the constitution both of religion and government.—SWIFT, *Sentiments of a Church of England Man.*

Let any man examine a reasonable honest man of either side upon those opinions in religion and government which both parties daily buffet each other about, he shall hardly find one material point of difference between them.—SWIFT, *Examiner*, *No.* 15.

CONTENTS.

* This Chapter is marked VI. through mistake, and the error is continued.

CONTENTS.

CONTENTS.

CONTENTS.

ERRATUM.

In page 110, third line of Chap. XIV. for "at the history," read "at the *early* history," &c.

ERRATA.

Page 57, line 8, for "undisputed," read "undecided."
59, line 20, for "selicet," read "scilicet."
224, line 6, for "vertus," read "virtus."

☞ TO CORRESPONDENTS.
The Author's post-town is Ballincollig.

EPISTLE DEDICATORY.

People of Great Britain and Ireland,

To you I dedicate the following pages. I do so because you are interested in the subject. You are, generally speaking, either Protestants or Roman Catholics; for I do not take into account those individuals, if any such be among you, who are so presumptuous as to reject Christianity altogether; and Protestants I account all such as, notwithstanding some discrepancies respecting ceremonies and matters of small importance, agree in admitting the great fundamentals of religion, and in rejecting what are considered the absurdities and superstitions of the Roman Catholic ritual.

The object of the following tract is, if possible, to restore among you the happy reign of religious harmony and brotherly love, or at least to narrow the grounds of religious strife and contention.

The well-informed Catholics abjure many ridiculous tenets and reject many silly observances, that prevail among the ignorant of their communion; and, therefore, in this respect, approach the confines of Protestantism. It appears that the English and Scotch Roman Catholics may, for the most part, be enrolled in this class; and that they are strangers to the superstitions that have taken such deep root and are nurtured in this portion of his Majesty's dominions. What inference is to be drawn from this fact? It must be admitted, of course, that the English and Scotch Catholics are orthodox; in which case, it follows, that Irish Catholicity, such as I have alluded to, is a deviation from genuine Catholic orthodoxy. What then is to be done? Should not Irish Catholicity be reformed, and be assimilated to that of England and Scotland? Does not Catholic uniformity, as well as the sanctity of religion, require this? Or are its corruptions to be perpetuated, and to be extended to England and Scotland? We do not think, from the present state of society, that this latter alternative will take place. The Roman Catholic religion, then, as far as these three kingdoms are concerned, is in an anomalous state, and at variance with itself. Even in this country, without crossing the Irish Channel, it presents a somewhat similar picture. The higher orders of the Roman Catholics differ more on the score of religion from the lower orders, though they all frequent one common place of worship, than from their Protestant brethren. How is this evil to be remedied? The remedy is in the hands of the enlightened Catholics of the three kingdoms. Will this superior class take no steps towards the enlightenment of the ignorant and uninstructed? Or if, through the perversity of churchmen, things are suffered to remain in *statu quo*, will they who profess the Catholic religion in its purity, as it is supposed, be content to be classified under one common appellation with those who make profession of it, overloaded with all manner of superstition and extravagance?

Further, what are the Catholic Priests of

England and Scotland, who exhibit the Catholic religion in its genuine form, to think of their brethren, the Roman Catholic clergy in Ireland, under whose guidance and instruction it is totally disfigured and disgraced? Is it not the duty of the former either to effect the reformation of the latter, or to repudiate their communion altogether? It is this vulgar, this corrupted Catholicity, which brings Irish Catholics and Protestants into deadly conflict with each other; that gives life and activity to sectarian bigotry and rancour. If this was put down or exploded, the Catholics of this empire might be classed with mere Dissenters from the Church by law established; in which case, there would be, what may be considered almost tantamount to religious communion, a general and a charitable recognition of one common Christianity. People of Great Britain and Ireland, if even so much were effected, would it not be a great blessing? I am endeavouring, at considerable risk, to act my part in this important work. I am labouring, amid good report and evil report, to assimilate and reconcile; to establish a sort of concordatum between conflicting religionists.

Religious rancour has produced a disastrous state of things in Ireland; and must prove, through Ireland, a drawback on the general interests of the empire. The Treatise, therefore, which I dedicate to you, is employed on a subject, in which you are *all* deeply interested. I do not attack the Catholic Religion properly understood. I war only with the spurious additions that have been made to it; with the extravagancies that have crept into it; and the anti-social principles that have been engrafted on it. My object is to separate truth from falsehood, the good from the evil, the genuine from the adulterate; in a word, to extricate religion and morality from the fangs of error and superstition, extravagance and fraud.

Britons, be assured that Ireland will not be pacified, nor will the empire enjoy internal repose, until the Catholic religion in Ireland undergoes this necessary purification. How this may be accomplished is the great point to be considered. As the matter in question is a national concern, it should, methinks, of right be taken up by the Legislature. What, if the Roman Catholic Prelates and Dignitaries of the three kingdoms were called together, suppose in London or Dublin, for the purpose of eliciting from them an authoritative and explicit declaration on this great subject. The first point for determination should be the identity of the Roman Catholic religion, as it is professed throughout these realms? This point being established, the abrogation or abolition of the pernicious peculiarities of the Irish Catholic religion or Catholic Church, must follow as a corollary. All this would imply, in the first place, that these same peculiarities are no part or parcel of the Catholic religion, contrary to the prevailing notions in this enlightened country; secondly, that the Irish Catholic clergy should signify the same to the people; and thirdly, that any and every clergyman, who may refuse to comply with this injunction, and still continue to countenance or sanction these peculiarities, should be interdicted, as a Catholic clergyman the exercise of his priestly functions.

There is every reason to presume that the Roman Catholic bishops and clergy of England and Scotland, who are, for the most part, unacquainted with the religious extravagancies of the Irish, would act a fair, open, candid, unequivocal part on the occasion. We opine also, that the Irish Catholic hierarchy, notwithstanding all the sins they have now to answer for respecting religion and morals, would furnish individuals ready to co-operate, in this useful work, with their brethren of England and Scotland; and, considering the matter altogether, it should be hoped, on such an awful occasion, under the present circumstances of Christendom in general, and of this empire in particular, that the cause of truth and purity would gain the undisputed ascendant.

Besides a decision on the palpable superstitions and absurdities of Irish Catholicity, the council should be called on to declare, whether or not the doctrine of passive resistance to law, such as was preached by the late Dr. James Doyle, and is almost every where inculcated on the people by their priests—a doctrine which has occasioned the perpetration of the most horrid outrages, and has led principally to the present deranged state of Irish society—whether or not this doctrine, so pregnant with evil, be in accordance with the principles of the Catholic religion? Also, whether the Irish priests acted the part of Christian ministers in marking out as objects for popular persecution, all such as kept aloof from, or did not co-operate with them in their anti-tithe combination? Further, as the lower orders of the Irish Catholics think themselves justified in hating and injuring those who differ from them in religion, the council in question should issue general instructions on this head, and make it imperative on the inferior clergy, to labour incessantly for the removal of this most pernicious error. It would be also incumbent on this council to declare, whether, according to the principles of the Catholic Church, priests are warranted in prostituting the functions of their ministry to the spirit of political faction, and in announcing to their congregations from the pulpit and the altar, that the great question of their eternal salvation or damnation, turns upon their voting, at parliamentary elections, for this or that particular candidate? Finally, this council should pronounce a solemn decision on the question of religious intolerance, that is, a juridical condemnation of the doctrine of Dens, and all such as have written like him on that mischievous anti-social subject.

This council should also be an open one, or

partly so. What I mean is, that Protestants should be allowed to appear there, and to state their difficulties and their objections. Full and entire satisfaction should be given to the public upon doctrines and principles, in which proximately or remotely all are concerned. Indeed, the Roman Catholic hierarchy, particularly of these kingdoms, should be glad of the opportunity, which would be thus afforded them, of laying the sure foundation, not only for the correction of local abuses—that is, for regulating what may be amiss in the internal concerns of their church—but also of clearing up doubts and difficulties to the satisfaction of an anxious community, and of giving such explanations altogether, as may exhibit their religion in its true and proper shape. For the denial of plausible or well-founded charges by unauthorized individuals is of no weight whatever, which would not be the case, if the denial or demurrer, proceeded from the assembled representatives of the ecclesiastical body.

People of the united kingdom, the welfare of Ireland requires that this or some similar experiment should be made. It would be a great point, if the Catholic religion in this empire were made to exist in its least objectionable form; a point not to be accomplished but by likening the general Catholicity of Ireland to that of England and Scotland; by identifying the respective hierarchies as to discipline and public instruction; by restraining the Irish Catholic clergy, like their brethren elsewhere, to the functions of their ministry; and by elevating the general body of the Irish Catholics to the same level of religious improvement with the well-informed amongst themselves, and with the mass, high and low, of the English and Scotch Catholic congregations. If, after this, it should be found, that the religious peculiarities of the British and Irish Catholics consisted merely in a few speculative tenets, having little or no relation to the intercourse of social life, or the interchange of social offices, the natural consequence would be, that harmony and brotherly love, a moral union, in short, would thenceforward subsist among all classes of religionists in the British empire.

People of Great Britain and Ireland, I have, in conformity with the prevailing sentiments and the spirit of our constitution, given an indefinite extension to the principles of religious liberty and religious forbearance. Indeed, speculative doctrines, either negative or positive, that is to say, doctrines that merely regard the state of things in the world to come, should not be subjected to human constraint or domination; which should only be brought into action when individual or public injury may be justly apprehended. Diversity of opinion in matters of religion, since it has ever existed all the world over, seems in some sort natural to mankind; to flow, indeed, from the existing order of things. Any gratuitous system, therefore, of counteraction, or of enforcing uniformity, is indefensible; and should be considered as opposed to the very disposition of Providence, both in regard to the human intellect and to the objects of human investigation. Philosophers and theologians may labour to enlighten the world by their knowledge, their discoveries, their reasonings, and their elucidations, and it is their bounden duty so to do; but their auditors, or their readers, should be moved or influenced solely by the force of argument and the power of persuasion. It should be admitted that a Unitarian may be as sincere in his belief as one that subscribes the thirty-nine articles, or professes the creed of Athanasius, or rejects the divine institution of Episcopacy, or maintains transubstantiation. But if Unitarians, or Church-of-England men, or the followers of the Kirk, or the sticklers for Roman orthodoxy, should labour to propagate their peculiar doctrines by the infliction of pains and penalties, they would, respectively, merit the execration and vengeance of mankind. Great doubts, notwithstanding solemn oaths and protestations, still hang over Roman orthodoxy in this particular. It is high time to have all these doubts satisfactorily removed. In short, the people of these realms have a right to demand, from the British and Irish Catholic Hierarchy, a distinct rejection of the principles of religious intolerance, and a distinct recognition of the principles of civil and religious liberty.

People of Great Britain and Ireland, you are in every respect the greatest civil community in the world. But unless the Irish Catholic Church, now so deformed and so mischievous, undergoes the necessary process of purification; unless it is purged, improved, reformed, reconstructed, your fame will be tarnished, and your glory incomplete.

I remain,

Your Fellow Subject and Citizen,

DAVID O'CROLY.

OVENS, November 1st, 1835.

PRELIMINARY DISCOURSE.

The following work has been principally occasioned by the strange part which the Roman Catholic clergy in this country have been acting this time past. The writer, who himself was one of that body, entered his protest from the beginning against their proceedings and their principles. He had imagined that the church taught submission to the law, as well as the love of one's neighbour, without distinction of religion. But the doctrine of passive resistance, which has converted Irish Catholicity into Antinomianism, and declared a war of extermination against the Protestant Church establishment, makes him somewhat doubtful on the subject.

He was so weak as to imagine, at the outset, that the Irish Catholic Bishops would take their stand at the opposite side, but he soon found that he had reckoned without his host; and that the priests of all ranks, high and low, were linked together in the same lawless confederacy. He, however, stood firm, and uninfluenced by the example of others, would not compromise his principles. He refused to grant the use of his chapels in Courcy's country, to Sir

Emmanuel Moore, who all on a sudden had become a fiery patriot, and an anti-tithe agitator. This circumstance proved the signal for a popular outcry against him. The baronet triumphantly quoted the authority of Dr. Doyle, just as the devil is said sometimes to quote scripture. His own curates took their stand in opposition to him; but yet at the side of their bishop and brother priests. They even headed his deluded congregation, and set his authority at defiance. He laid a statement of the case before the Ordinary; who sent him a whining, milk and water answer; insinuating that he had brought all the troubles on himself, by having shown, first of all, such backwardness in the collection of the Catholic rent, and such hostility latterly to the collection of the O'Connell tribute; adding the common cant of agitation, that the people were warranted in their *constitutional* resistance to bad laws. All this showed the animus of the man.

Vexed with the ill requital which he thought he received from the people of Courcies, whom he had faithfully served for nearly ten years, he availed himself of an opportunity that offered, of negociating an exchange of parishes; when, leaving Ringrone, he took up his residence at the Ovens, as parish priest of that district. Here similar difficulties and similar troubles, arising from similar causes, awaited him. His new curate, whom it is unnecessary to name, was a violent anti-tithe agitator and bigot, and extremely ignorant withal. This hopeful ecclesiastic, who, like many of his fraternity, was ever ready to justify or palliate all the excesses of popular fury, laboured incessantly to undermine his authority, and misrepresent him to the poor people, denouncing him as leagued with their enemies, and, under the existing state of popular excitement, placing his very life in danger. He made up his mind to bring matters to an issue. He sought to get rid of this refractory curate. For this purpose, he lodged a formal complaint against him, on the score of his having advanced principles subversive of the morality of the Gospel; which commands us to injure no man, but on the contrary to love and assist one another. The Ordinary took no notice of the complaint, nor even deigned to answer the letters of the complainant. Yea, more, he took this preacher of pure morality by the hand, became his patron and protector, gave him authority to act without any reference to his parish priest, and exercise an independent jurisdiction. This was at once to sanction the propagation of pernicious principles, to encourage insubordination, to violate ecclesiastical discipline, to invade individual rights, and to authorise the unjust seizure of the parish revenues. But every thing was considered lawful or justifiable that might exasperate or subdue the man, who presumed to have an opinion of his own; and to be the advocate of law and order in opposition to his Bishop and diocesans. To effect this laudable object, every thing was overlooked, and unheeded—sound principles, order, discipline, justice, and fair dealing.

When, from a personal interview with the Ordinary, he received a confirmation of all this, he resolved to withdraw from the jurisdiction of so iniquitous a superior, and to dissolve his connection with a body, from whom he was already severed in principle. He resigned his parish, (not however with the necessary formalities,) and retired with the intention of never returning to his former unnatural association or subjection. His will, however, in this respect, after a lapse of some time, was overruled. At the pressing instance of some respectable parishioners, to whom he acknowledges himself indebted, he opposed the introduction of a new parish priest, and claimed the right of resumption on the ground that he had never made a canonical surrender. The demand, after much debate and altercation, was conceded—accompanied, too, with a promise that the obnoxious curate should account for his receipts, and be immediately removed. But the promise was not fulfilled. The curate remained in the parish for above three months, still pursuing the same course, still exercising an independent jurisdiction: neither was he compelled to settle his accounts; and when at length he received the long promised route, he was permitted by his bishop to go off with all * * * * * *

Hic multa desiderantur.

A new curate was appointed, who understood very well that he was at full liberty to imitate the example of his predecessor, to give similar annoyance, and to assume similar prerogatives. All this too was eagerly anticipated; but the anticipations were not realised. This honourable man gave up for the moment the service of O'Connell, and acted in unison with his parish priest. In short, he disappointed his patron, and, like a virtuous minister of the Gospel, preferred his duty to his interest.

This, comparatively speaking, was a period of respite; occasioned, however, not by any change of system in the head and members of the priesthood, but by the good disposition of an individual, who was removable at will. As to the public at large, outrages were checked by the terror of the coercion act; but priests and people, pastors and their flocks, or more properly speaking, the followers of O'Connell, retained the same sentiments and dispositions, religious and political; and were prepared, as occasion may require, for new feats of agitation and turbulence. The parish priest of the Ovens still stood singular and alone; his relative position was unchanged. He could not venture with safety on the dangerous task of removing the errors or changing the dispositions of his congregation; or of teaching them the duties they were bound to discharge as Christians, as subjects, and as members of civil society. He was still maligned by the bigot, lay and clerical, because he lived on friendly terms with his Protestant neighbours; while his trusty friend the bishop still inveighed bitterly against him, because he showed no willingness to prevent poor children from attending the Oven's parochial school—a school which merits the highest commendation, which meddles not with questions of religion, which teaches no catechism, even to the Protestant children, for they are regularly taken from it to the parish church, to be catechised; and which, but that priestly hostility overawes the poor people, would be well attended and prove a blessing to the neighbourhood all round. The character, indeed, of its patron, the Rev. William Harvey, is a guarantee against any impropriety in the establishment. Under these circumstances, the parish priest published his essay on ecclesiastical finance, &c. &c.

This publication, which animadverted severely enough on the course pursued by the Irish Catholic priesthood, both as to religion and politics, and on that system of agitation, which tends at once to impoverish and demoralise, gave mighty offence to the whole faction of Connel, lay and ecclesiastical. The essay, also gave the opinion of the author as to the amount of agreement in essentials of the two religions, and that the main points of difference turn upon accidentals, or upon matters which may or ought to be dispensed with. This brought at once about his ears the bishop and the priests; who lost no time in denouncing the essay as teeming with damnable errors, although it contains no doctrine that has not been maintained by Roman Catholic theologians ; and in denouncing the author as a base apostate, deserving fire and faggot, though he merely echoed the sentiments of Dr. Doyle, on the supposed differences in religion ; and sentiments likewise, to which he himself formerly gave public expression without incurring any note of censure.* He was cited peremptorily to appear in Cork before the Ordinary and his council ; that is, before judges, who had already condemned the work, and made no secret of their determination to punish the author. He was cited also when every thing had been said and done to exasperate the multitude against him ; and among whom the report was all at once circulated that he was coming to the city to stand his trial. His friends became alarmed for his personal safety, and advised him for the present not to quit his own house in the country. The proceeding against him was savage and bloodthirsty. He did not therefore answer the citation as required ; but he apologised—stating the fears he entertained for his personal safety, yet expressing his willingness to answer any question that may be propounded to him in a place of privacy and safety. He requested that a confidential person may be sent to his own

* Vide " The Address to the Lower Orders" ad finem.

house for that purpose. This request was refused; and without further citation—contrary to canon law, which requires three—he was served with a letter of suspension; which suspension was to continue in force, until a retractation would be made of a number of condemned propositions, which, it was pretended, were extracted from the offensive publication. This was to pass judgment with a vengeance; and shows clearly enough what was to be expected from so vindictive a tribunal. He demurred to the proceeding on the score of informality. This produced a new letter from the Ordinary, containing at once a new citation, which he authoritatively said should stand for three; and a new suspension, or as he said, a supplement for any informalities in the former. The author wrote a respectful remonstrance, again alleging the well-grounded fears he had of making his appearance in the city, and repeatedly requesting a conference in a place of safety. But all from the beginning was time and labour lost; the thing was plain enough; his destruction, as far as his enemies could accomplish it, was resolved on. Besides being suspended, his temporalities were seized on; and though a month elapsed in this doubtful state, before he was formally deprived of his benefice, no restitution of the portion to which he was entitled has been made since.* But this is

* Vide Appendix No. 2.

just in keeping with the pecuniary transaction already recited; and is a sort of elucidation of what is stated in the essay "that church revenues among the priests in many instances are a mere scramble." But let us bring to a conclusion this tedious and tiresome narration. The 16th of November 1834, closed the scene. On that day the Rev. James Daly, or Dawly, was formally inducted and installed as the new parish priest of the Ovens—a radical from the school of O'Connell; "Porcus de grege Epicuri." After which induction, about three in the afternoon, a letter was delivered from the Ordinary to the now ex-parish priest, dated the day previous, stating that he the Ordinary had given orders for the proceeding that had already taken place*—a very suitable termination to as arbitrary and uncanonical a process as ever took place in any matter of similar import; but which has produced the salutary effect of re-establishing uniformity throughout the diocese; and preventing the parish of the Ovens from being any longer an exception to the general rule. It was well for the author that he lived under the protection of British law.

We come now to the general question. The object in part of our former essay was, if possible, to approximate the two religions, and to establish Christian concord between conflicting sectaries.

* Vide Appendix No. 3.

Resting upon facts and admitted doctrines, we thought the idea may be entertained. We ventured to draw a distinction between the religion taught by priests and the superstitions inculcated by friars. But it appears the distinction was gratuitous and not at all warranted by fact—that priests and friars are indeed in perfect unison; are cemented together; are one and indivisible; and that what was sacrilegiously called consecrated trumpery belongs to Irish Catholic orthodoxy. In this view of things the essay writer erred, both as to theory and to fact. However, he is not willing to abandon the subject, and therefore he now respectfully presents to the public a critical examination into the chief points of controversy between the two churches.

Ignorance and error on this important subject prevail to a great degree among the multitude. And how could it be otherwise when priests and friars—their accredited instructors—have entered into an unholy combination to keep them in darkness; and even to persecute any individual who may undertake to enlighten them? But the good work is not therefore to be given up. Some attempt must be made to counteract the evil. Perhaps the following pages may prove serviceable in this particular, may awaken a spirit of enquiry, may excite suspicion, may create a wholesome distrust, may assist in guiding the multitude to form a true estimate of men and things, may, in fine, by the exposition of imposture and the refutation of error, dissolve the spell of bigotry and superstition, and prepare the way for the ultimate establishment of true and unsophisticated Christianity in this unhappy country. This task is praiseworthy ; it is the same with that of the Baptist, " To give light to them that sit in darkness, and to guide their feet into the way of peace."

CHAPTER I.

INTRODUCTION.

THE author of the "Essay, religious and political, on Ecclesiastical Finance," has drawn down on his head ten-fold vengeance by that publication. His character has been assailed by every species of vituperation. He has been placarded, lampooned, reviled and calumniated. He has been deprived of his temporalities, and his very life put in jeopardy. All this, too, has been done by persons calling themselves Christians, and with the sanction, and more than the sanction, of those who profess to be ministers of the Gospel. This was to act an unbecoming part. It was also bad treatment of a man, who contemplated nothing but what was good —namely, to improve the condition and manners of the Catholic Clergy, and to lop off from the Catholic religion acknowledged excrescences—excrescences, which by no means improve its appearance, and render it extremely objectionable in the eyes of many. The accomplishment of all this would do infinite service to the cause of religion in general; and, what is greatly to be desired, improve the state of Irish society.

He gave a detail of well-known abuses, with a view to their correction—abuses the joint offspring of a bad system and the weakness or perversity of human nature. This exposé, however offensive it might prove, was demanded by the important subject he took in hand. No individual was criminated; nor, properly speaking, was the body aspersed. Startling but undeniable facts and usages were stated, which operate greatly to the prejudice of religion and morality in this country. He touched incidentally on some points of religion to show, that Protestants and Catholics ought not to be so ready to quarrel with one another on that score. He did not say much on the subject; yet the little he did say is made the pretext for all the injuries that have been heaped upon him. He now enters more fully into this important question.

CHAPTER II.

There is no priest, whatever may be his bias or stupidity, who must not acknowledge, that very ridiculous ideas on the subject of religion prevail among the uneducated portion of the Roman Catholic community. How these notions have been imbibed, or have originated, it may be difficult exactly to ascertain. The presumption is, that the clergy themselves—the directors and instructors of the multitude—had a principal share in the transaction. But whether this was the case or not; from whatever source the evil flows, whether from clerics or from laics, or from both, it is the duty of those, to whom the religious instruction of the people is committed, to apply the proper remedy—to labour for the removal of religious error and the establishment of religious truth. This is the duty of the present generation of the clergy, without any reference to the past. But, unfortunately, it is a duty which they have not yet begun to perform. On the contrary, as will be shown hereafter, the whole drift and tendency of their preaching and their example is, to perpetuate all the religious errors and prejudices that have been handed down through ignorance or knavery from generation to generation. The priests appear to think it lawful for them to sanction in public what they ridicule in private; imitating, in some sort, the Pagan Hierophantes of old; of whom Lactantius says, "Et quod adorant in templis ludunt in theatris." It is this pernicious system of sacrilegious connivance, that enlarges the ground of difference between the two churches, and contributes to array Catholic and Protestant in deadly hostility to one another.

CHAPTER III.

The author of the essay has been condemned for asserting, that the Catholic and Protestant religions do not differ so widely from one another as some people imagine; and that between the enlightened of both classes there are not many shades of difference. This is a serious question and worthy of consideration. Undoubtedly we should make a distinction in the Catholic body; who are by no means to be viewed, even as religionists, all in the same light; but, on the contrary, should be separated at least into two classes—the enlightened and the ignorant; the creed of the former being much less extensive than that of the latter, and by consequence approximating or inclining to Protestantism. If then it be proposed to compare or assimilate the two religions, which class should we exclude or which should we press into our service? The answer is obvious.

But let us see first of all, whether the question of religious assimilation should be entertained; or whether there are, in reality, essential or irreconcilable differences between the two religions, properly considered. This question would be easily disposed of, if we were to decide from the *present* temper and conduct of the Irish Catholic Clergy—men who now affect to shrink with horror from all contact with Protestantism, and doom to perdition the impious individual that dares to apologize in its behalf; who, in short, stand up in defence of Irish Catholicity in its most enlarged acceptation, with all its vulgar appurtenances and appendages. But we are of opinion that these high-toned gentlemen—bishops, priests and friars though they be—are, in their present outre position, very questionable authority in religion as well as politics; and that they are nothing more or less than innovators on genuine Catholic orthodoxy. We must have recourse to other and less exceptionable authority. Let us begin with the late celebrated Doctor Doyle, who was held in such high estimation by the Roman Catholics of this country. We quote, as we have already done elsewhere, from his letter to Mr. Robertson on the practicability of a union between the two churches. "This union, (says he,) is not so difficult as appears to many. It is not difficult, for in the discussions which were held, and the correspondence which occurred on this subject early in the last century, as well as that in which Archbishop Tillotson was engaged, as the others which were carried on between Bossuet and Leibnitz, it appeared that the points of agreement between the churches were numerous, those in which the parties hesitated few and apparently not the most important. The effort which was then made was not attended with success, but its failure was owing more to princes than to priests, more to state policy than a *difference of belief.* I would (continues he) presume to state, that if Protestant and Catholic divines, of learning and a conciliatory character, were summoned by the crown to ascertain the points of agreement and difference between the churches, and that the result of their conferences were made the basis of a project to be treated on between the heads of the churches of Rome and of England, the result might be more favourable than at present would be anticipated. The chief points to be discussed are, the canon of the sacred scripture, faith, justification, the mass, the sacraments, the authority of tradition, of councils, of the pope, the celibacy of the clergy, language of the liturgy, invocation of saints, respect for images, prayers for the dead.

" On most of these it appears to me that there is no essential difference between the Catholics and Protestants. The existing diversity of opinion arises in most cases from certain forms of words which admit of satisfactory explanation, or from the ignorance or misconceptions which ancient prejudices and ill-will produce and strengthen, but which could be removed." Thus far Doctor Doyle. His language on the subject is clear, explicit, decisive. He declares for the practicability of church union. He says, that the failure of former attempts did not arise from the nature of the question, but from accidental circumstances. He enumerates the points at issue, and he roundly asserts that, in regard to most of them, there is no essential difference between Catholics and Protestants; and he believes it quite possible to remove every diversity of opinion, if proper means were employed; that is—if due explanations were given, and the matter committed, on both sides, to men of moderation, learning, and discernment. Hear ye this ye Catholic, or rather ye anti-Protestant population of this country. Listen to the words of your favourite bishop, of him whom ye were wont to regard as an oracle, or as a second St. Paul. Ye listened when he preached to you the doctrine of passive resistance; and why not catch from his lips the hallowed, the consoling doctrine of religious union and assimilation? What has the author of the obnoxious essay done more than to echo this bishop's sentiments; to echo them, indeed, for the second time? For when his letter to Mr. Robertson first made its appearance, the author already mentioned announced at once, through the medium of the *Cork Mercantile Chronicle*, that the sentiments and views of the Doctor met with his full and unqualified concurrence.* It may be here remarked that Dr. Doyle, though a friar of the Augustinian order, in enumerating the

* Vide address to the lower orders—Appendix.

points for discussion, says not a word of scapulars, habits, cords, &c. &c., as if he considered such things unworthy of one moment's consideration. But not to stray from the subject. Dr Doyle in this matter merely copied after the great Erasmus, who was of opinion, that the differences and distractions in religion, which prevailed in his time, regarded, for the most part, matters that did not belong to the essence or substance of religion. In his 107th letter, which is addressed to Prince George of Saxony, he acknowledges that, when Luther appeared, the world was lulled asleep with scholastic opinions and human ordinances, that nothing was heard of but indulgences—which were given for money—and the power of the Pope! In his letter to Pope Clement the 7th, congratulating him on his accession to the Papal dignity, he exhorts his holiness to use his influence and authority in putting an end to the troubles and disorders occasioned by differences in religion. This, said he, might be done, if the sovereign Pontiff would alter all those things that might undergo alteration without injury to religion. He even submitted a plan for effectuating this great object—namely, "that the King of France and the Emperor should unite together for the establishment of the truth; that from all the various nations of Christendom, one hundred and fifty persons should be selected, pious, learned, and judicious; that their conclusions or decisions should be summed up by a smaller number, deputed or appointed for that purpose; that many useless questions debated in the schools, should be discarded; that some ecclesiastical precepts should be abolished, and others changed into counsels; that the churches should be provided with pastors fit to instruct the people; that, in fine, the discipline of the Church should be observed, and religion be made to flourish in its pristine purity." This language of Erasmus—the greatest scholar and theologian of his time—is very apposite and very edifying. Have we quoted sufficient authorities for our purpose? We have on our side Bossuet, Leibnitz, Tillotson, Erasmus, and the redoubted Dr. Doyle. We might swell the list with the names of Melancthon and the other divines—Catholic and Protestant—who were present at the conferences of Augsburg; where all extraneous matter being thrown aside, the two religions were nearly identified. We may also quote on our side a multitude of authorities, among which are found the immortal names of Grotius, Hooker, Courayer, and Swift. All these authorities, and particularly that of Dr. Doyle, should make a deep impression upon the considerate portion of the Irish Catholics, and dispose them to give the right hand of fellowship to the followers of that religion which is fairly acknowledged to possess, as well as the Roman Catholic, all the great essentials of Christianity. So much for the general question.

CHAPTER IV.

We now enter into a comparison of the two religions. It may not be amiss to quote again a few words from Dr. Doyle. "It appeared (to Bossuet and Leibnitz) that the points of agreement between the churches were numerous; those upon which the parties hesitated were few, and apparently not the most important." It would appear from these words, that in the mind of the Doctor, Protestantism and Catholicity are nearly convertible terms, having indeed in common the same inspired writings, the same God, the same Saviour, the same Lord Jesus, the same Apostles' creed, the same Baptism, and in a great degree the same form of divine worship. But this is Catholic theory, between which and Catholic practice what a difference!!!

As to the points of disagreement, (to speak in general,) it would appear to follow, from what has been said, and what is admitted, that they do not appertain to the essentials of religion. This seems to be the opinion on the side of the Catholics; and yet these same non-essential matters keep the two churches asunder and in a state of mutual hostility. Why are they retained by the one, and why are they rejected by the other? Where does the fault lie? Protestants ground their rejection on the charges of superstition or falsehood; in which case the thing becomes a matter of conscience; whilst on the other hand, the admission that the points in question are non-essentials, implies that they may be abandoned "Salva fide," or without affecting the integrity of religion. Taking this view of the case, it is unnecessary to specify which party is to be condemned.

Protestants complain that the simplicity of religion or of Christianity, as it was originally preached and propagated, has been departed from; and that the Roman Catholic church lends the sanction of her authority to many errors and superstitions. The professed object of Protestantism is to get rid of these objectionable appendages; and, agreeably to the proposal or recommendation of Erasmus, to make religion flourish in its original purity. What is the true mode of accomplishing this great object? Is it not by instituting a comparison between the past times and the present, and endeavouring to ascertain what was taught and practised in the first ages of Christianity? But it is time to come to particulars.

CHAPTER VI.

OF THE BIBLE.

DIFFERENCES exist on the subject of the sacred Scriptures. Both churches indeed agree on the general question, as to their inspiration, and to their paramount authority in matters of religion. Both are agreed also as to the utility of their perusal, but disagree as to the mode or manner—the Protestant church allowing the indiscriminate use of the Sacred Volume, whilst the church of Rome clogs with certain conditions the privilege of its perusal. With the latter, indeed, the question is one of expediency. There is besides no uniformity among them in this particular; the result perhaps of individual indolence or caprice. Some bishops allow a greater latitude than others; but in Ireland, for the most part, the perusal of the Bible is represented as pregnant with danger, and by no means encouraged.*

A difference of opinion exists as to the number of canonical books. Several that have been placed in the canon by the council of Trent, are numbered by the church of England among the Apocrypha.

* Appendix, No. 2.

It must be admitted that on this point the Protestants have antiquity on their side. Their canon of the Old Testament corresponds with that of the Jews, to whom the Old Testament was committed, and who never admitted among the inspired writings the book of Tobit, or of Wisdom, or the story of Bell and the Dragon, or the book of Judith, or of Ecclesiasticus, or the books of the Maccabees. It appears clearly enough also, that the earliest fathers coincided in opinion with the Jews on this subject, and consequently were Protestant pro tanto—so far.

It may be remarked that there is not a direct clashing of opinion between the churches on this question. Although the councils of Florence and Trent have inserted these books in their canon of the Old Testament, Catholic theologians do not scruple to draw a marked line of distinction between them, and the books that were ever acknowledged as canonical. They make a distinct class of the former, and denominate them Deutero-canonical; thus limiting them to a sort of second-rate species of inspiration.

Concerning the use of the Scriptures much has been said and argued these three centuries past. It is well known that the discipline of the Roman Catholic church was for many ages directly hostile to the dissemination of the Sacred Volume, or the publication of it in the respective vernacular languages. The Latin vulgate, which, notwithstanding its numerous errata, received the irrevocable stamp of authenticity from the council of Trent, was the only version in general use throughout the Latin churches previous to the Reformation. Before that period, the use of the Bible was confined to those who were skilled in the learned languages. The scriptures were, in regard to the community at large, what the Holy of Holies in Solomon's temple was, in regard to the Jewish multitude.

The vulgar herd was forced to keep aloof.

Richard du Mans, a Franciscan friar, maintained, in the Council of Trent, that as the Christian doctrines were sufficiently explained by the schoolmen, the reading of the Scriptures was quite unnecessary for the laity—that none but professed theologians should be accorded that license ; for that Luther's proselytes or followers were generally made up of such as had habituated themselves to the perusal of the Sacred Volume. It is probable the good man was not aware that, in thus expressing himself, he pronounced a high eulogium on the doctrine of the great reformer—that he was, in fact, announcing its conformity with the revealed word. Erasmus was censured by the faculty of divines, in Paris, for having ventured to assert, that leave to read the scriptures should be indiscriminately granted.

The reformers, resting their dissent from the Roman Catholic church, upon the principles contained in the Bible, were extremely forward in publishing versions of it in the various languages of Europe. When Henry VIII. abolished the pope's supremacy in England, a new English version of the scriptures was soon put in circulation. Wickliff, indeed, had already set the example. A new state of things had now commenced in regard to the Holy Scriptures. The Roman Catholic church copied in some measure the example of the reformers. Affairs in religion took a strange turn. Though the Reformation was incomplete, its effect was universal. It wrought a general revolution in the minds of Christians. The majority, indeed, adhered to the religion of their predecessors, and continued to reject the tenets of the evangelical preachers: but, notwithstanding this adherence, they were still averse to the system of putting a seal on the sacred writings. A general curiosity was excited to explore the hidden foundations of religion. It would, therefore, have appeared suspicious in the church of Rome, and made her seem to distrust the merits of her own cause, if, under such circumstances, she denied all access to the divine volume. Moreover, she deemed it necessary to publish what she called faithful versions, in order to counteract the evil effects that may result from the corrupt translations of daring innovators: for an alarming outcry was raised against the versions of the reformers; though it is well known that they were the best linguists of the time, and principally contributed to the revival of literature.

Orthodox vernaculuar translations now appeared in most of the countries of Europe, accompanied by large prefaces and elaborate comments. It was considered dangerous to suffer the word of God to go alone and unaccompanied among the people. Its obscurity, its mysteriousness formed the grand theme of declamation. Some craggy passages of St. Paul, which the labours of the Council of Trent could not smoothen, were urged as a demonstration, that the Scriptures were not designed for common use, or to be read at all without the aid of an approved commentary; as if the obscurity of some passages cast a shade on the entire, or that a few dark enigmatical texts should operate as a bar to the perusal of what is plain, intelligible, and edifying.

The Protestant plan of circulating the Scriptures without note or comment is condemned. But is it condemned upon good grounds? We ask, was it right for the Jewish people to listen to the discourses of Jesus Christ? Was it dangerous for them, was it to run the risk of imbibing error, to hear from his lips, without gloss or comment, those maxims, precepts, doctrines, parables, which have been committed to writing by the evangelists, and have been handed down from generation to generation for the perpetual instruction and edification of mankind?

The holy fathers unanimously recommended the

perusal of the Scriptures. They never assumed the liberty of representing a book, which is the foundation of religion, as pregnant with all manner of religious difficulties and dangers. St. John Chrysostom in his homilies and sermons never failed, with all the force and fervor of his eloquence, to impress on the minds of the people the obligation they were under of studying and digesting the contents of the evangelical and apostolic writings. All the other fathers concurred with Chrysostom. How dissimilar is the conduct of the Roman Catholic bishops and priests in this country? After turning the whole kingdom topsy turvey on the subject, they have banished from the schools the New Testament, lest, of course, it may contaminate the poor children, and set them, even before the development of their faculties, upon the serious and difficult work of dogmatizing in religion—apprehensive that young Paddy Shaughnessy or young Darby Twoomy, who have not yet attained the age of puberty, may, by having the New Testament put into their hands, be prompted to institute an immediate inquiry into the propriety of clerical celibacy, or raise questions on the two-fold procession of the Holy Spirit. They are guilty, too, of inconsistency and partiality in this matter. They exclude the English Testament from schools, yet allow the Greek and Latin Testament to be read there. But this privilege is accorded only to a few; and the evil forsooth is not worth notice, because of the smallness of its amount. This is a very bad salvo. Further, after a desperate struggle for complete exclusion, the anti-Biblicals have at length permitted selections from the Old and New Testament in the vernacular language to be put into the hands of little ones—thus running a zig-zag ridiculous course in regard to the question altogether. The generality of the poor people, owing to their anti-Biblical instructors, are fully persuaded that the Bible is a book of doubtful character, is a religious ignis-fatuus, calculated or adapted to decoy the world into all the mazes of error and extravagance. What is this but to malign the Holy Spirit and to impugn inspiration?

CHAPTER VII.

TRADITION.

TRADITION, about which so much has been said and written, is a mere non-entity in religion. It is called the unwritten word; and may be denominated a sort of supplement to the New Testament. It is supposed to be a portion of revelation, which was not committed to writing, but continues to be delivered orally as at first; and has been transmitted in this manner from age to age down to the present time. Hence the term "Tradition." Now, the great point to ascertain is, what this traditionary revelation contains; what dogmata it teaches; what precepts it inculcates; what particular maxims it recommends in contradistinction to the written word, or to the writings of the evangelists and apostles in the New Testament? Has the church, at any time during the eighteen centuries of her existence, placed before the world in a tangible shape, or in due form, this grand section of the revealed word? Has she ever ventured to define or determine it either in whole or in part? She has done nothing of the kind. The apostles and evangelists did not mark it down; the first fathers followed the example of the apostles and evangelists, they slurred it over; their successors, in like manner, passed it heedlessly by; councils that were assembled of every description, general and particular, took no notice of it, and thus has it travelled down to our days without shape or form—a sort of spiritual essence unheeded, unperceived, untouched, undefined and undefinable; and this is to form an essential part of religion!!! Tradition is a mere figment—a vanum sine se nomen—an empty name: much like what is called the treasure of the church; which, according to our metaphysical theology, is made up of the superabundant merits of Christ and his saints, and on which she is pleased to draw occasionally in behalf of poor sinners, among whom she distributes it in the pleasing and consoling form of "indulgences." And yet this tradition, this consecrated phantom, this shadowy substance, is magnified into a reality, and made one of the great grounds for erecting a wall of separation between Christian brethren and believers. But will this weak point continue to be insisted on? Will the Roman Catholic church refuse to enter into terms of peace and amity when she is not called on to make any *real* sacrifice? We shall see more on this subject hereafter.

CHAPTER VIII.

INFALLIBILITY.

From what has been said on tradition, it appears that the Scriptures of the Old and New Testament are the only authentic source whence to deduce the word of God revealed to mankind. Further, it is admitted that no new or additional revelation has been made; that the word delivered by Christ and his apostles should remain unchanged and unaltered, without addition or diminution, to the end of time. This important admission is made by all parties amid endless contradictions arising from the actual state of things. Hence again it follows that whatever appertains or is peculiar to Christianity must rest for support solely and exclusively on the written word. The great point then to ascertain is, what are the doctrines contained in the Sacred Volume, and what the duties it inculcates. The Roman Catholic church, or rather the episcopal body, assumes a very high privilege in this particular. They affirm that they inherit from the apostles, whose successors they claim to be, a divine commission to expound the word of God and determine its meaning; and that, in pronouncing their solemn decision on the subject, or on disputed points of religion, they are surely and infallibly guided by the Holy Ghost. The common belief of Roman Catholics is, that their bishops possess absolute infallibility—that is, without bounds or limitation in matters pertaining to religion: as if, indeed, they possessed the privilege of extending or contracting its dimensions according to their own good will and pleasure; whereas infallibility, if the term is to be used at all, can only apply to that which really and truly constitutes the Christian doctrine or dispensation.

Half-witted theologians who appear to be sticklers for indefinite infallibility, argue the point in a very cavalier manner. It may not be amiss to advert a little to what they say. The Roman Catholic bishops are successors to the apostles; ergo they are infallible; or they constitute an infallible church. In this enthymeme we may grant the antecedent and deny the consequence. For the bishops who separated from the church of Rome on account of her supposed errors, derived their succession equally from the apostles. Ergo they are infallible, or they constitute an infallible church. In this case we should have a number of contradictory infallibilities. The Greeks are infallible as well as the Latins, and the Protestants may lay claim to the same supernatural prerogative.

The church is said to be the immaculate spouse of Christ, without spot or wrinkle, "tota pulchra," all beautiful. She is therefore infallible. It would be a great happiness if the hierarchy, and the great body of Christian believers, presented, in their carriage or demeanour, a form of this heavenly description. But unhappily, such is the perversity of human nature, that the visible church exhibits a very different appearance. It is composed indeed of good and of bad; of wise virgins and of foolish ones; of the reprobate and the righteous. The church then may be contaminated by moral turpitude, and yet be immaculate. Yes, it will be said, the morals of its members may be corrupt, but their creed is immaculate; that is, contamination is not the effect of vice, but of speculative errors. This is a reductio ad absurdum.

They argue in favour of indefinite infallibility,

from the words of Matthew, chapter xvi. v. 18, "Upon this rock I will build my church, and the gates of hell shall not prevail against it." But what in reality did Christ mean by the promise here given? The gates of hell or death shall not, said he, prevail against my church; that is, it shall not be overcome or extinguished by the multitude or power of its enemies; it shall be established never to be subverted, or Christianity, like the sun in the firmament, shall endure until time shall be no more. But he could not mean that perversity, in the shape of vice or error, should never find its way into the church; for we know that in both ways it has been disfigured and deformed. Let us examine another text.

"Go ye," says, Christ to his apostles, as we read in the 28th chapter of St. Matthew, "and teach all nations—teaching them to do all things whatsoever I have commanded you; and lo! I am with you all days to the end of the world." When he was about to quit this life, and return to the bosom of his Father, he commissioned his appostles to preach and propagate the Gospel; that is, to perfect the work which he himself had begun. He commissioned them to teach all nations, all without distinction, Jew and Gentile; and lest they may tremble at the contemplation of so arduous an undertaking, and to assure them of success, he promised them his own uninterrupted assistance and co-operation to the very end. The apostles were about to commence a work of inconceivable magnitude—to batter down, without any ostensible means, the solidly constructed fabric of pagan superstition; few and unprotected they were to set themselves in opposition to the combined world, by labouring to subvert the religions of all nations without exception. To effect this the actual interposition of God's power was essentially requisite; and therefore, the apostles, agreeably to the promise of their Divine Master, were accompanied by his power, which was manifested in the signs and wonders they performed; and by his enlightening Spirit, which was displayed in their energy, their zeal, their knowledge and their doctrine. This interpretation agrees with the corresponding or parallel text in the Gospel according to Mark, who makes the promised accompaniment of Jesus Christ to consist in the miraculous powers that signalised the preaching of the Gospel. See also St. Luke, chapter xxiv. v. 49.

But it is alleged that Christ spoke to the successors of the apostles, as well as to themselves; for that the apostles were not to have their existence prolonged to the end of the world. The Greek words, of which "the end of the world" is a translation, may be interpreted "the termination of life," that is, the termination of the lives of the apostles, and the nature of the promised accompaniment, which was to be miraculous, restrains the words to this sense.

Christ bound himself in the most solemn manner to aid and assist his apostles without relaxation or interruption to the end, in the great work of preaching and propagating the Gospel; which pledge he has to all intents and purposes redeemed. To refer his promise equally to after ages is to bestow on his words an interpretation which neither the usage of language, nor the subsequent state of religion will warrant. It will be granted, we should suppose, that the successors of the apostles at the present day, as they style themselves, are not endowed either with miraculous powers or the gift of inspiration. Our present Catholic and apostolic bishops, unless some Hohenlohe appeared among them, would hardly venture to lay hold on serpents, or quaff the poisoned bowl. There are no prophets now in Israel. How are these frail and powerless successors included in the promise made by Jesus Christ to his apostles? He is with them, but they cannot tell how. He promised to be with his apostles after one manner, and with their successors after another. This is indeed to make the most of the text. It is nothing more or less than to manufacture two promises out of one—quite contrary to an axiom of the old metaphysicians—non sunt multiplicanda entia sine necessitate.

He accompanies them, it is said, in their doctrinal decisions. In council assembled the bishops are infallible, are inspired by the Holy Ghost. There they decide like apostles. " As it seemeth right to the Holy Ghost and to us." Great words, magnificent pretensions; and which seize forcibly on the imaginations of the simple and unreflecting; who indeed are taught to consider their bishops in council as an assembly of supernatural beings; and to revere their decisions as the very dicta of the Holy Spirit. The bishop of Bitonto, in his discourse to the fathers of Trent, compares them to the council of the gods described in the *Iliad* of Homer. But whoever is well acquainted with the history of the church will easily perceive that in all ages these bishops, as well in council as out of council, bore on them all the marks of human perversity, frailty, infirmity and imperfection. Let any man of a sound, unprejudiced mind read the proceedings of these Christain bishops and clergy on the successively controverted doctrines of Arianism, Nestorianism, and Eutichianism, the latter of which followed the former as an effect from its cause; let him read the cabals, intrigues, violences, and animosities, that were fomented and exercised by these Christian bishops in their councils of every description, small and large, provincial, national and universal; let him read of their varying formulæ and their varying creeds; their condemnations and their approbations; their subscriptions and their retractations; let him force his way, if possible, through the confused heap or chaos of the church synodical decisions of the fourth, fifth and sixth centuries—decisions that embroiled the Christain world, and so distracted the minds of men that they knew not what to credit or disbelieve; let him view this jumble of contradictions, discrepancies, wickedness and nonsense generated by Christian bishops, and say, if he can believe these same bishops, under any circumstances, whether congregated or dispersed, to be surely and infallibly guided by the inspiration of the Holy Ghost. "*Credat Judæus Apella.*" St. Basil, whose conclusions were drawn from facts and experience, did not hesitate to affirm that councils of bishops or ecclesiastics only increased the divisions in religion, and, by their intemperate proceedings, made every thing worse instead of better.

But let us pursue our argument; let us reason from concessions and from facts. It is said that council definitions or canons are conclusive or *de fide*, though we are admitted to dispute the goodness or validity of the reasons assigned. Whoever calls in question the former is anathematized; but we may controvert the latter without incurring the charge of heterodoxy. All this is odd enough, but it is a concession that must be made. For the weakness, or insufficiency, or nullity of the reasons assigned as a warranty for their definitions by the fathers in many councils assembled is so glaring, so palpable, that the most accomplished

Sorbonist with every subtlety of argument would find it impossible to extricate himself from the labyrinth in which he would find himself involved, were he to maintain, that their arguments as well as their conclusions should be received as truths of revelation. What convincing reasons the fathers of the second synod of Nice employed to revive and re-establish the doctrine and usage of image worship! Legends, romances, fabrications were the premises whence they drew their conclusions. To shew that the worship in question was practised from the beginning and originated with Christ himself, they adduced as a certain truth the apocryphal narrative given by Evagrius—how Christ sent his own picture or likeness as a present to Agbarus, the pretended king of Edessa. For the same purpose they alleged also an idle story then in currency, that the woman whom Christ healed of an issue of blood erected a statue to his memory. In the fourth council of Lateran, the canons and constitutions shaped and introduced by Innocent the Third, were acquiesced in by the accommodating Fathers without even the formality of a previous discussion, though Matthew Paris says, that a diversity of opinion existed respecting their merits or expediency. This was to decide without assigning any preliminary reason. In the councils of Perpignan, Pisa and Constance, the reasoning of the fathers was, for the most part, the language of faction, intrigue, jealousy and passion. At Basil the adherents of the pope were vigorously opposed by the sticklers for council authority, and the respective fathers came to an open rupture. At the Council of Trent the system of management was admirable. In order to prevent dangerous discussion among the inspired members the questions were first of all decided in private congregations or committees; and then introduced to the Council, not to be discussed anew but to receive final ratification. Every thing at this council was managed so completely, according to the directions and will of the successive popes, that it used to be said of the post-boy who travelled with instructions from the Vatican to the presiding legates, that he carried the Holy Ghost in his mail-bag or budget. But to proceed. The reasoning of the fathers in council may be questioned, but their conclusions or definitions must receive implicit belief. This is strange logic. You are at liberty to deny the premises, but you must grant the conclusion. We presume it will be admitted that the fathers in council argue in due form, that they do not transgress the rules of reasoning laid down by Aristotle, that they do not deal in sophisms. For if they were to argue inconclusively, or expose themselves to the charge of sophistry, it would be something like an absurdity to say, that they were under the influence of heavenly inspiration. But then, if they argue justly, and fairly, and logically, how can we be warranted in denying their premises and granting their conclusions?

Again, either the conclusions follow from the premises or not. If the former, we may reject them or examine them *de novo;* if the latter, why investigate at all? In this case to be borne out we must suppose the good men to be actually inspired, and inspired very unfortunately too, without being enabled to give any proofs of inspiration, save the deficiency or imperfection of their reasoning faculties!! To be consistent, they should cast investigation aside altogether, since they are left to mere human resources in the process of it; and without any jumble of things human and divine, as undoubted inheritors of apostolic gifts and privileges, define out of hand all the component parts of Christianity.

Let us adduce some facts that are directly opposed to the received notions of infallibility. Numberless falsehoods and errors and superstitions are, it is admitted, bound up with the religion of the Roman Catholic church. She orders a portion of what is called the Roman Breviary to be daily recited by the clergy under the penalty of mortal sin, a volume rejected by the Gallican church, and abounding with fables. This is to corrupt with falsehood the fountain-head of religion. She sanctions in like manner the circulation of similar books of *pseudo* devotion among the laity; for example, the prayer-book of the "sacred heart;" which contains certain silly forms of devotion, founded on some pretended revelation made some years ago to an old French female enthusiast or impostor. Look at some of the church festivals—one instituted in honour of the immaculate conception, which St. Bernard said, was first got up by some hair-brained idiots; another in honour of the pretended brands of St. Francis, a most ridiculous legend; and a third, to commemorate the scapular of Simon Stock. Of this last more hereafter.

Let us glance at the ages before the Reformation; and see what falsehood and nonsense were incorporated with religion, when the Roman church was in the hey-day of her infallibility. The church at that period either knew nothing of criticism, or she practised imposition on the world. Witness the supposititious works of Dennis, the areopagite, which are still recognized by the Breviary; the canons ascribed to the apostles; the false decretals; all which, and many more apocryphal writings, she held up to the world as genuine and authentic. It was ignorance, or a spirit of deception in this matter that procured credence for feigned miracles and pretended revelations, performed and announced so frequently during the middle ages, that the laws of nature seemed to have been established for no other purpose but to be suspended. Then did the white friars, and grey friars, and black friars, and preaching friars, and friars of all colours and qualities—the proclaimers of wonders—make their appearance. Then did innumerable corps of ecclesiastical militia, oddly and fantastically equipped, marshal themselves for religious warfare, to combat, as they said, the devil, the world, and the flesh, each regiment receiving its standard from above, accompanied by a suitable number of gifts, graces, miracles, and revelations.

Then did the most learned of the Christian doctors apply themselves to the most silly, unmeaning, unintelligible religious disquisitions. Petrus Lombardus learnedly examines whether Jesus Christ, *quatenus* man, be a person or a thing. Whether the Father begot the Divine Essence ; or the Divine Essence begot the Son ; or whether one essence produced another ; or, finally, whether the essence be neither produced nor producing ? Scotus published folios of religious nonsense. St. Bernard, in his 345th letter, directed to the monks of Anastasius, very gravely asserts, "that if any of them chanced to be ill, it would not be allowable for them to use any remedies, save common herbs—that it was contrary to the spirit of religion to buy drugs, employ physicians, or take medicine. This saint was no great friend to doctors or apothecaries.

It was principally during this period of church enlightenment that the Breviary, of which we have already spoken, was stuffed with ridiculous legends ;

in which are paralleled all the vulgar tales concerning apparitions, miracles, wells, charms and incantations, that get currency at all times among the ignorant and credulous multitude—a proof that the clergy of those times were fully possessed of opinions or errors, which, long since exploded by the revival of true religion and philosophy, are now confined to the most illiterate and superstitious portion of mankind. Where was papal infallibility, or church infallibility, slumbering all this time?

How does this wonderful attribute show itself in regard to the Holy Scriptures? Does it show itself either in the text or in the interpretation? In neither. St. Jerome acknowledges that the Latin Vulgate, the version in common use before his time in the western churches, was teeming with errors. This indeed was the reason why that learned man undertook to give a new version of the Old Testament from the original Hebrew. What became of church infallibility in this particular? It was the great learning of St. Jerome—the result of his talents and his labour, that corrected the sacred text, and supplied the deficiency of the church in this important particular. Let us proceed. The Scriptures contain many obscure, difficult, perplexing passages. Perhaps infallibility is here brought into play. No such thing. It shows itself neither in the translation nor in the explication; but ill-naturedly leaves to eternal cavil and disputation among all sects and parties a considerable portion of the divine word.

Does this infallibility ever show itself in regard to morality or casuistry? Not at all; for there are cases innumerable in which doctors differ:

> "Grammatici certant et adhuc sub judice lis est."
>
> Doctors dispute; one this, one that maintains,
> And undisputed still the thing remains.

There are numberless cases in which the pro and con, the for and against, this or that opinion are respectively supported with equal plausibility. Let those who have leisure and patience read over the treatises on casuistry, on right and wrong, compiled for the use of Roman Catholic seminaries, and they will perceive the cloud of uncertainty in which common practical cases are irretrievably involved. What then shall we say of this mighty attribute—church infallibility? It does not regard the Breviary, which deals so much in romance; nor the Missal, which contains many things that are apocryphal; nor the Calendar, which stands in great need of revision; nor suppositious books in religion, which have been in all ages, and even still are in general circulation; nor the Sacred Scriptures, which were not always preserved in their original purity, and many parts of which remain still unexpounded; nor even the Moral Code, which taken in its full and comprehensive extent, is rendered intricate and obscure. This indefinite infallibility therefore is, like the unwritten word, nothing but a mere chimera. Infallibility, if we are to make any use of the term, is applicable only to religion—without any reference whatever to this or that particular denomination of Christians—the saving truths and maxims of which are preserved in an imperishable record—the sacred writings—a record the divine origin of which is admitted in common by all.

One word more, and we shall conclude this part of our subject. The question of church infallibility is, according to Roman Catholic principles, an open one. No general council has decided on it, no definition respecting it, ending with an electrifying anathema, has been yet announced to the world—a remarkable circumstance, considering that it has been so much impugned. But how could the thing be otherwise? For the definition of her infallibility by the Roman Catholic church would necessarily presuppose the very thing to be defined—a sophism that would drive Aristotle into hysterics.

CHAPTER XI.

THE SCRIPTURE THE ONLY SURE FOUNDATION.

It is very natural that a book, which all classes of Christians acknowledge to be divine, should possess the greatest authority in matters of religion. This is the case with the scriptures of the Old and New Testament. On the canon there is indeed some difference of opinion. To every good critic it appears plain enough that the books rejected by Protestants are of doubtful authority; and that the church had existed for centuries before these same books were called canonical. Even so late as the seventh century we find that Gregory the Great looked upon the two books of Maccabees as apocryphal. "These books," said he, "may be read for instruction, but not to prove any mystery of faith." Gregory, indeed, only follows St. Jerome, the great translator of the Bible, and the highest authority on this subject. His words are, "*Sicut ergo Judith et Tobiæ et Machabæorum libros legit quidem ecclesia sed eos inter canonicas scripturas non recipit sic et hæc duo volumina, selicet Ecclesiasticum et sapientiam, legat ad edificationem plebis, non ad auctoritatem ecclesiasticorum dogmatum confirmandam.—Sancti Hier. præfatio in libros Solomonis.* "Like as the church indeed reads the books of Judith, and Tobit, and the Maccabees, but receives them not among *the canonical* writings; so she may read these two books (Ecclesiasticus and Wisdom) for the instruction of the people, but not to confirm the authority of church dogmata." It is, indeed, very strange that the Jewish apocryphal books should become canonical in the hands of Christians, and that too in opposition to the recorded opinions of the most learned fathers. The genius of Protestantism seems to be to admit of nothing uncertain in religion; and, therefore, it strictly adheres to the canon of the Jews respecting the books of the Old Testament.

It does not appear, however, to observe all this strictness in regard to the canon of the New. The epistle to the Hebrews, that of St. James, of St. Jude, as also the Apocalypse, were balanced for a considerable period in the scales of public opinion, and gave rise to many contradictory criticisms before they received the final stamp of undisputed canonicity. In latter times, indeed, Luther rejected the epistle of St. James; but in this he has not been followed. This facility of admission on the part of Protestantism cannot be displeasing to the Catholic Church; which, however, is still greatly dissatisfied because it does not make much larger concessions.

Tradition, or the unwritten word, of which we have already spoken a little, is not admitted by

Protestants. It is rejected *a priori*, because of its uncertainty. Its advocates argue very plausibly, when they speak in general terms, or argue in the abstract; but they are strangely perplexed when they come to particulars. They are utterly at a loss to specify any distinct tenet, or precept, or maxim, that was made the subject of a revelation, distinct from the written word; so that, when they come to details, every thing is vague, indefinite and uncertain. They contend for an unwritten word, but know not in what it consists. Their general argument merely amounts to this, that Jesus Christ and his Apostles said many things which were not committed to writing—a proposition that must be admitted. But it is very unlikely, when so many sacred pensmen, all under the direction of the Holy Spirit, undertook to write down the doctrines and precepts of the new covenant, that they executed this great task in a garbled, imperfect manner; that they omitted any truth which should be believed, or any precept that should be practised. Doubtless the revelation delivered was not so bulky or so complicated as to require to be cut into two portions, and not to be committed to writing in toto without any extraordinary trouble or inconvenience. The Gospel contains many repetitions, and details circumstances comparatively trivial. Matters, therefore, unnecessary and of minor importance, were registered in this divine book, and some essentials omitted. The supposition, too, is gratuitous; for the writers of the New Testament say nothing of this two-fold revelation, nor give the slightest hint that any essential truth of religion was overlooked in their writings; and finally, this extraordinary supposition is made by those who are completely at a loss to assign what portion of revelation remained unregistered, or was committed separately, to the uncertain fate of oral tradition.

Catholic divines themselves have virtually given up this point; have abandoned the unwritten word as a mere phantom of the imagination. They endeavour now to establish all the principal points of their religion by the authority of the written word; in which case the question is decided as to the nullity of any other separate body or portion of revelation. The signification of the term itself—tradition—is changed when applied to theology; for it means nothing more than the opinions of the ancient fathers, and the various definitions of ancient councils on questions of religion and church discipline. So that the "word" itself expressing this supposed separate portion of revelation is ambiguous and equivocal. Thus much for the question *a priori*. Let us now view it in reference to consequences.

There is no doubt that if the Scriptures had been always held in view, it would have tended to preserve religion in its original simplicity. A deviation from this rule has given it a new aspect altogether. There are innumerable items in the Roman Catholic religion, which have no warranty from Scripture. It would be an endless task to descend to all the particulars. Protestant divines are not all exactly agreed on this question. The disagreement merely regards the amount of ecclesiastical institutions or innovations. It would be no easy matter to justify, by warranty of Scripture, the use of beads, rosaries, scapulars, cords, *agnus Deis*, habits, and of many other matters of a similar description; or the forms and manner of addressing the Blessed Virgin or the other saints; or the addition to the scripture canon; or the complicated doctrines concerning the mass or the celebration of the Lord's Supper; or the multitudinous ceremonies that have been gradually engrafted on that simple institution; or the worship of images, relics, consecrated oils, and the consecrated elements in the holy sacrament; or monastic institutions; or vows of celibacy and unlimited obedience; or pontifical jurisdiction; or reservations of sins, or jubilees, or indulgences. All these, and many more great additions and embellishments of religion, would be wanted to Christian people, if a steady eye had been ever kept on the simplicity of the gospel.

But the establishment of all these extraordinaries was highly favoured by the supposition or the doctrine, that an unwritten revelation was committed to the custody of the church; or rather to the holy keeping of the church hierarchy. The unwritten "word" could not remain barren and inoperative, but should act its own part and produce its own peculiar fruits amid the sum total of Christianity. We have, therefore, first a complicated revelation, and then, of course, a complicated religion.

Let us not, however, be misunderstood. We do not mean to insinuate that all the peculiarities of the Roman Catholic religion are given to the world as the offspring of the "unwritten word." Many of them are referred to more recent authority, but yet equally divine. The history of the Roman Catholic Church is filled with records of special revelations—not indeed by all believed—which have given rise to innumerable religious institutions and regulations. To be satisfied on this head, it is only necessary to consult the orthodox breviaries, the lives of saints, the histories of the various religious orders, the scapular book, and the famous church of Loretto. There are many other books of a similar description, but these are quite sufficient for our purpose. The unwritten word, therefore, which is supposed to have had existence in the time of the Apostles, has been prodigiously augmented by successive subsequent revelations; and, indeed, it may well be said that the condensation or aggregate of the entire has had a much greater share in the formation of the vulgar religion than the unquestionable revelation transmitted to us in the writings of the Evangelists and Apostles. Protestants reject, with every show of reason, the whole foundation of this extravagant superstructure—condemning the modern reveries or impostures as altogether ridiculous and revolting—and will admit of no religion but what is conformable to the undoubted word of revelation.

CHAPTER X.

OF THE SUPREMACY OF THE POPE.

They who maintain that the Bishop of Rome is head of the church, and to be obeyed as such under all circumstances, must be prepared also to maintain his infallibility; for otherwise even unjust or sinful commands would imply an obligation of obedience. The doctrine, however, of papal infallibility is quite unfashionable at the present day. To suppose that he is the centre of unity, or that all churches should of necessity be in communion with the church of Rome, comes exactly to the same thing. For if we suppose that the particular church of Rome, or the bishops of Rome, fell into error and remained obstinate, it would, in such case, be imperative on other churches to separate themselves from her communion. The doctrine, therefore, of papal infallibility, though rejected in terms, is still admitted by implication.

This opinion, which is still expressly maintained by the ultra-Montanists in opposition to the Gallican church, (which latter does not, however, deduce the necessary consequences of their denial,) was, in former times, for many ages the received doctrine of the Latin churches. The great schism of the fifteenth century, which distracted western Christendom, and presented the western church in the form of a three-headed monster, like the dog Cerberus, somewhat changed the ideas of Christians on the subject. Then the doctrine of papal infallibility was denied, though upheld by the prescription of ages. The Gallican doctors hold that a council is superior to the pope; while the Italians, on the contrary, hold that the pope—their own grand dignitary—is superior to a council. The synods of Constance and Basil, if suffered to go on, would have considerably abridged the prerogatives of the Roman pontiff. The publication of the spurious decretals at an inauspicious time—when Christianity was at a low ebb and the tide of ignorance at a frightful elevation—in a great measure raised the Roman pontiff on the shoulders of Christendom. Then did he assume all power, and consider the nations as his inheritance. But the state of Christendom and of the human mind underwent, in progress of time, a change for the better. Learning revived together with the art of criticism. The imposture of the decretals was detected; and the detection proved to the Christian world, that the magnificent pretensions of Peter's successor rested upon a sandy foundation.

The first bishops of Rome were very moderate in their pretensions. It does not appear that St. Peter, who is called the founder of the Roman see, possessed more authority than St. Paul—his fellow-labourer. It is not necessary to discuss the question whether or not St. Peter was ever at Rome. We hear nothing that can be relied on concerning the headship of Linus and Clement. When Polycarp, bishop of Smyrna, paid a visit to Pope Anicetus, for the purpose of consulting with him as to the proper time of celebrating the Christian passover, the two holy bishops treated each other as equals. Polycarp officiated publicly in place of Anicetus; and when they could not agree on the subject of their consultation, they parted with the utmost cordiality—having mutually agreed that each should in this matter observe the custom of his own church.

It is true that Pope Victor, in the following century, deserting the example of Anicetus, ventured to excommunicate the Asiatic bishops for refusing to adopt the Roman custom as to the time of celebrating Easter. But his excommunication was disregarded. The bishops of Greece and Asia Minor—of Ephesus, Corinth, and the various dioceses in Judea,—made no scruple to resist him to the utmost. Separately and in council they defended their own custom and persisted in its observance. The conduct of Victor shews that he had lofty pretensions; but the effectual opposition he encountered proves that he exceeded the limits of his authority.

The dispute as to the validity of baptism by heretics, which took place in the third century between Pope Stephen and Cyprian, bishop of Carthage, proves that the pope's authority at that period was rather circumscribed. The bishop of Carthage never subscribed to the papal definition, though he laid down his life for the gospel. Nor was the definition of the pope received in the East, no more than in Africa. It is, indeed, supposed that Stephen fell into an error opposite to that maintained by Cyprian. In the church of Alexandria for many years after, the baptism of heretics was considered invalid, and their discipline was regulated accordingly.

In the early councils, the bishop of Rome did not preside. The greatest questions were moved, discussed, and defined, independently of his peculiar concurrence, or the exercise of his all-controlling authority. In the account we have of the apostolic council of Jerusalem, we cannot discover that Peter occupied any superiority of position over the other apostles. He spoke; so did several others; but James dictated the decision of the council. It may be remarked that the apostles at Jerusalem, when they understood that Samaria had received the word of God, sent down Peter and John, in order to pray that the new converts in that city may receive the Holy Ghost. This transaction makes exceedingly against the sovereign authority of Peter.

In the council of Antioch, which condemned the heresy of Paulus Samosatenus, the Roman pontiff had no share. Pope Sylvester did not preside in the first council of Nice, either in person or by his legates. That office was filled either by Hosius, bishop of Corduba, or Eustathius of Antioch; which latter is denominated chief bishop by Proches and Facundas. It is more probable, however, that the former presided; for Athanasius entitles him the father and president of all the councils. His name, too, occupies the first place in the list of the subscribing bishops. It is no where mentioned by the ancients that he acted as the pope's deputy on the occasion. Gelasius Cyzicenus, a modern, was the first who made the unauthorised assertion.

The sticklers for papal prerogative, fully aware how prejudicial to their cause it would prove were it believed that the pope did not take a leading part in the first general council, sought how to prevent so serious an evil. For this purpose the system of fabrication was resorted to. A synodical letter from the council to Pope Sylvester, together with his reply, was framed and put into circulation. The work of fabrication did not stop here. As the pope did not preside in the council, nor was present there, it was judged right that the decisions of it, in order o their validity, should receive his seal and confirmation. It was necessary to give things a modern press. Accordingly, we find, upon spurious record, that a council was assembled at Rome by papal authority of equal respectability in point of numbers with the council of Nice, in which the acts of the latter received the final and irrevocable sanction and approbation of the Holy See. The fabricators of this precious portion of "tradition" thought themselves ingenious; but they have only proved themselves to be confounded bunglers. To pass by the direct proofs of the forgery, the thing has nothing about it of verisimilitude. If the pope presided by his deputy, what subsequent confirmation was necessary on his part? And nothing can be more silly than the supposition that the acts of a general council required for their validity the confirmation of a petty ecclesiastical convention.

The sixth canon of this council is worthy of remark. It runs thus—"We order that the ancient custom shall continue to be observed, which gives the bishop of Alexandria jurisdiction over the various provinces of Egypt, Libya, and Pentapolis, just as the bishop of Rome possesses over the suburbicary districts." They had no idea then of the pope's universal supremacy.

In the third council of Constantinople it was ordained that the bishop of that capital should thenceforward hold the next rank to the bishop of Rome; or that he should be considered, as to dignity, the second bishop in the Christian world. And because all these abridgments and extensions of jurisdiction were the consequence of accidental circumstances and ecclesiastical arrangements, and liable, of course, to change and alteration, we find that the jurisdiction of the Alexandrian bishop, which had been so extensive as, besides Egypt, to comprehend Libya and Pentapolis, was, by a canon of this council, confined within the limits of the Egyptian frontier.

Cyril of Alexandria, the active enemy of Nestorius, presided in the council of Ephesus held against that patriarch. The legates of Pope Celestine were present, yet Cyril presided; and though some of the ancient fathers gave him the title of the pope's deputy, they do not mean that he acted in that quality as president of the council. He is indeed thus entitled, because, after the condemnation at Rome of the doctrine of Nestorius, at the instance and representation of Cyril, and the deposition of the unfortunate man himself, the execution of the papal sentence was entrusted as a matter of course to the bishop of Alexandria. The legates were commanded to act in conjunction with him. But these representatives of the pope had no share in the presidency of the council. Even when Cyril ceased for a time to fill the chief place—having dwindled for a moment into the humble form of a petitioner, the pope's legates still acted a subordinate part; and Juvenal, bishop of Jerusalem, assumed, *pro tempore*, the presidency of the council. Cyril presided, because, together with his high character, he was in point of rank the most honourable patriarch present; and if the pope himself had attended the council, he would, perhaps, for the same reason, have occupied the presidential chair.

At the second council of Ephesus, held by order of Theodosius, to examine the affair of Eutiches, who, improving on the doctrine of Cyril, maintained an opinion apparently opposite to that for which Nestorius had been condemned, Diosorcus, patriarch of Alexandria, presided, the second place of honour being occupied by Julian, the legate of Pope Leo. The same business was subsequently revised and re-examined in the great council of Chalcedon, held by order of the emperor Marcian; at which the imperial commissioners appear to have presided or kept order—concluding and deciding according to the votes and declarations of the attending ecclesiastics. The twenty-eighth canon of this council elevated the patriarch of Constantinople—the *new Rome*—to an *equality* of rank with the bishop of *old Rome;* conferred on him equal honours, equal distinctions, and equal privileges; and all this because Constantinople had become the new capital and seat of empire. Its ecclesiastical jurisdiction had been progressively on the increase from the days of Constantine the Great, when the imperial seat was translated thither. This canon encountered strong opposition from the pope's legates. But in vain. It was received and ratified.

Where then are all these divine, hereditary, indefeasible rights of papal supremacy? Why are ecclesiastical arrangements denominated divine institutions? St. Peter was not superior to St. Paul, nor Anicetus to Polycarp. The greatness of the Roman city gave dignity to the Roman see. In the early ages, the church of Rome must have been beyond all others numerous and respectable. Rome, until the uprise of Byzantium or Constantinople, was, for size and population, infinitely beyond any other city in the Roman world. The bishop of such a city must have taken a leading part in all great ecclesiastical affairs. Hence the boldness of Victor, and the doctrinal definition of Stephen. Had a bishop of Rome been present at the various councils of Nice, Ephesus, and Chalcedon, he would probably have presided, for the Roman see was considered the most honourable. The pope's legates were, therefore, always highly respected, and greatly influenced the council decisions. Nevertheless, the bishop of Rome was not considered in any other light than as bishop of the greatest see. The Roman church was not the mother and the mistress of all other churches. This idea was altogether unknown in the primitive ages. Neither the superintendence of the Roman bishop, nor his canonical summons for assembling, affected in any degree the validity or authority of œcumenical councils. The citation for convening proceeded from the imperial throne, and the presiding chair was filled by some extra-papal ecclesiastic. The increasing greatness of Constantinople raised up a competitor for dignity with the Roman pontiff; and the competitorship was rendered serious and permanent by the sanction of a council, which for importance and dignity has never been surpassed.

This infant exaltation of prerogative acquired more strength as it increased in years, and became continually more formidable to the antiquated claims of Roman primacy. The patriarch of Constantinople extended his jurisdiction in proportion to the increase of his prerogatives or the exaltation of his rank. The remonstrances of jealous Rome were unavailing; and she saw at length, with pain no doubt, but yet with submission, her conquering rival assume the pompous title of œcumenical patriarch. The easterns considered John the Faster to be superior in dignity to Pope Gregory the Great: and when the final separation took place, the seeds of which had been sown in the contest between the new prerogatives of Constantinople and the ancient privileges of Rome, all the patriarchs of the East, of Antioch, Alexandria and Jerusalem, adhered to the new primate, leaving the bishop of Rome solitary and alone an absolute, uncontrolled monarch to rule with an iron rod over the vast extent of his own proper patriarchate.

The prerogatives of which the popes were deprived by the eastern bishops, were, in a short time, counterbalanced with interest by the extraordinary augmentation of their isolated patriarchal authority. The bishops of the west became completely subjected to papal dominion. The rich and extensive territory, which was governed by papal authority, elevated the pope to the summit of pontifical power. He became the source, the centre, the focus of all ecclesiastical jurisdiction. The abbeys, monasteries, bishoprics throughout the Latin church were, in a great measure, at his disposal. The last appeal in ecclesiastical causes lay to the Court of Rome, where the final decision was pronounced. Interest at Rome was the sure step to promotion ; opposition from that quarter blasted every hope.

The vassalage of the Church involved states in the same calamity. The vast influence, which in virtue of his headship the pope possessed over the immense body of ecclesiastics scattered through the nations that owned his authority, rendered him a person of the highest interest in the eyes of kings and princes. His territorial possessions made his alliance a matter of some moment. Monarchs courted his favour and acknowledged his pre-eminence. He became the umpire and arbitrator between contending nations or contending monarchs. He disposed of regal crowns as he did of episcopal mitres. He ruled church and state with despotic authority, until at length, so great was the prevailing fatuity, that he was acknowledged to be the grand source of both civil and ecclesiastical jurisdiction.

The extravagant height to which the papal power was raised, contributed to hasten its downfall. The abuses, the exactions, the intrigues of the Roman Chancery at length filled Europe with disgust and indignation. The danger of so many liege subjects being under the control of a foreign protentate, was seriously felt by the respective governments. Opposition to the pope's will in the appointment of a solitary bishop was sufficient to subject a whole nation to the awful evil of an ecclesiastical interdict, to suspend the exercise of religious worship, to close up the receptacles of the dead, to spread religious terror through the land, and to array the fanatical people in arms against their Sovereign. The reigns of Henry the Second and his son John demonstrated to England the fatal effects of papal authority. The influence and authority of the pope gave dangerous confidence to Becket; and Innocent the Third had well nigh hurled John from the throne to support the pretensions of Stephen Langton.

It was the dignity appended to the papal see that gave stability to the great and scandalous schism of the fifteenth century. The respective pretenders to the papacy, when once in possession, or in supposed possession, were unwilling to resign such ample prerogatives. But their pertinacity made the existing evil more manifest. The gradual diffusion of critical knowledge, as well as the pressure of the evil itself, awakened people to a sense of the degraded state to which papal domination had reduced religion. All these causes concurred to lower the Bishop of Rome from his extraordinary height, and to prepare the way for the reformation, which has laid the axe to the root of all his dangerous prerogatives. To conclude this article—we repeat what we have stated elsewhere, and to which statement exceptions have been taken, that the question is one of discipline rather than of faith. Strip the pope of all his adventitious authority, or of that portion of it which is considered objectionable. Let him still be a patriarch; but let not his patriarchate be too extensive. Let him consecrate or appoint bishops, and exercise ecclesiastical jurisdiction in the provinces or dioceses round about his own territory; but let not his jurisdiction interfere with the independence of national churches. The doctrine of the Gallican church, which gives him little more than a primacy of honor, and this arising originally from the circumstance that Rome was the imperial city, comes very close to Protestantism on the subject, and removes at once, and by wholesale, the great ground for altercation on the subject.

CHAPTER XI.

ON CHURCH UNITY.

Having devoted a chapter to the Pope, who is called the centre of unity, let us now make some reflections on unity itself, as one of the marks of the Roman Catholic and Apostolic Church. By unity is understood sameness, or agreement, or coincidence in matters pertaining to religion. This mark is supposed not only to affect the church as she now exists in all her ramifications and extent, but also to characterise her past state in reference to her present, and will remain affixed to her as an holy badge of discrimination to all ages. The poor Roman Catholic people imagine that their church, like the Deity, is "the same yesterday, and to-day, and for ever."

That such a unity is in sublunary existence, taken in an enlarged sense, cannot be maintained. Great discrepancy, as well in the theory as in the practice of religion, is found both among the clergy and among the laity of the Roman Catholic Church. The religion of the secular clergy, at least as to outward appearance, differs from that of the regular; and, if past times be compared with the present, it will be found that religion is continually assuming new appearances. The friars have blended with religion a number of festivals and observances, and a variety of things that are neglected and even ridiculed by the secular priests. The former, however, attach, for weighty reasons no doubt, mighty importance to these consecrated peculiarities, and endeavour to give them all possible currency. They have, it may be said, the sole administration of a certain description of religion—if religion it may be called—which takes greatly with the lower orders. Scapulars, habits, beads, &c., are almost the exclusive property of friars. From friars also comes the largest share of indulgences—a species of spiritual merchandise about which there is a great diversity of opinion, even among the orthodox themselves. It was expected that the Council of Trent would have settled the question of indulgences—the very question too which brought Luther first into the field. But this expectation was not realised. The Council, for lack, perhaps, of due inspiration at the moment, left the matter as they found it. The practice of the church has, however, decided the question. Indulgences are constantly published, particularly by friars; and a jubilee, which is the plenitude of an indulgence, is occasionally proclaimed to the Roman Catholic world.

The vulgar belief is that indulgences or jubilees purge from every stain of sin. This, however, is the case only with the common people. The better sort set little or no value upon indulgences, but merely let the thing go on. In this there is nothing like unity.

There is an amazing diversity among the religious books that are published, and get circulation, even among those that are peculiar to the clergy, the Breviaries. The Parisian Breviary rejects a large portion of the Roman; which in like manner excludes from its pages considerable portions of the various and diversified Breviaries of the friars; and no wonder, for these last are stuffed with the most disgusting nonsense. The Roman Breviary too is different from what it formerly was. Some saints have been dislodged from the calendar; and many legends, which were formerly ordered to be read under the penalty of mortal sin, have been suppressed as apocryphal, or as being ridiculous beyond endurance. This is all right. It is the progress of knowledge and improvement. But it does not square well with the prevailing notion of church unity.

The prayer-books in common use have also undergone revision and improvement. The old fashioned ones would not be adapted to the present times, which may detect absurdities that passed unnoticed fifty years ago. Many silly prayers to the saints have been altered, many expunged; some old women's tales—revelations and miracles have disappeared. Yet much still remains to be done in this way. What was mother church doing in former times that these alterations and improvements became necessary? How came to pass these multiplied and successive changes—first of all for the worse, and then for the better? This is an odd kind of unity.

It was in the time of St. Bernard that the feast of the immaculate conception began to be observed in some diocese of France—an innovation in the calendar which gave great offence to that holy personage, who was styled the last of the fathers. He said it was got up by a set of hair-brained idiots. Nevertheless the festival gained ground, took root, was adopted by the Roman Catholic church, and maugre the idiocy of its origin still holds a distinguished place in the Roman Calendar and Missal. To this may be added the curious feast of the stigmata or brands of St. Francis of Assysium. The story of these brands, as related by Bonaventure, when first put into circulation, was almost universally ridiculed, as it is even now in private by those who labour in public to perpetuate the delusion. Its extreme silliness raised a considerable outcry against it. However, all this was counteracted by the pious industry of the Franciscans, who laboured successfully to consecrate a legend, which cast, as they thought, additional lustre on their sainted founder and patron. The brands of St. Francis have become part of the church office, even in the Roman Breviary and Missal. Does religion undergo no change by being thus incorporated with every thing fabulous and nonsensical?

The *stigmata sancti Francisci* are not to be found in the Parisian Breviary; which for this and similar other profane deficiencies is branded as a heterodox compilation, by the rigid votaries of the Portiuncula. Where is the unity in all this? But let us go on.

We have said elsewhere that the mass or the Lord's supper, as it was originally called, was, at the outset, celebrated in the most simple manner imaginable. Our Saviour took bread and wine; he blessed or gave thanks, and then distributed. This was the mode and manner of the institution, as may be learned from the three evangelists, Matthew, Mark, and Luke, and from the apostle Paul. There was no elevation of the host, no genuflections, no vestments, no complication or variety of ceremonies; and yet all must acknowledge that, amid this extreme simplicity, the celebration was in nowise maimed or defective. Little alteration was made during the lives of the apostles, who, according to Gregory the Great, merely added the recital of the Lord's prayer to the words of benediction or consecration. What changes and improvements have taken place in the lapse of eighteen centuries!! If the apostles should now revisit the world, and witness the gorgeous ceremonial of a pontifical mass, is there any possibility that they could identify it with their own simple celebration of the Lord's supper? If it be granted that the thing is the same, it must also be admitted that the appearances are *toto cœlo* different. And the sticklers for the mass must also allow that if the Protestant ceremonial was adopted, the thing would, in like manner, be the same, to say nothing of the stride that would thereby be made towards the simplicity of the original institution. There is no doubt that this remarkable change, if it has not affected the substance, has altered the form and complexion of religion, and cannot well be reconciled to the prevailing doctrine respecting church unity.

Indeed, religion in its whole frame and economy has assumed new forms and appearances. Baptism, like the Lord's supper, was very simple at the commencement. It would be difficult to prove that Philip, the deacon, when he baptized the noble Ethiopian in the stream on the high way, used consecrated oils and salt on the occasion. Yet the people of the present day would be very unhappy, and consider the rite itself extremely defective, if it were administered without these and a multitude of other adventitious accompaniments. Infant baptism is now universally practised, and this under the belief that the child who dies without baptism will never enter the kingdom of heaven. The practice of the first ages was different. Baptism was then, for the most part, administered to adults, who should also be first instructed in the rudiments of the Christian religion; and not indiscriminately at all times, but on special occasions. The hurry at present manifested respecting it has no warranty from the discipline of the early ages—a thing quite inexplicable, if we suppose that they viewed baptism exactly in the same light with the moderns.

It would be no difficult matter to trace the change that has taken place to the writings of St. Augustine against Pelagius on the subject of original sin, of which he says baptism is the remedy under the new covenant. This learned father, who was much addicted to metaphysical theology, and as he himself acknowledges—*Magnus opinator*—an adventurous thinker, gave rise, by his subtle disquisitions, to many novel opinions in religion. This is said of him by St. Hilary. But the Augustinian friars commend all his writings, and say, that he, above all others, explained and elucidated the doctrines of the gospel. It is now, however, pretty generally admitted that, before his time, little was said on the subject of original sin, or on the effects at present ascribed to baptism; nor is the reasoning or doctrine of this father so very feasible altogether. He endeavours to prove the existence of original sin by assuming that, in the old law, circumcision, and in the new, baptism, were instituted as the respective remedies for that spiritual evil. The theology of the schools objects not to the cleansing efficacy he ascribes to baptism; but his assumption respecting circumcision is rejected by all. The Israelites neglected this rite all the time they were in the wilderness, and the female portion of the community were at all times out of the question. He seems also to have forgotten that circumcision was not coeval with our first parents, but commenced with Abraham, according to the sacred writings. The truth is, that neither Abraham, nor Moses, nor the prophets, understood original sin as it afterwards existed in the mind of Augustine; nor the successive remedies which he ventured to particularize: neither, if we are to judge from the then prevailing discipline, did the Christians of the first centuries consider baptism, like the moderns, as a rite of uninterrupted indiscriminate necessity. It was when Constantine the Great was at the point of death, that he was baptized by Eusebius, the bishop of Nicomedia, the great protector of Arius.

It was administered originally by immersion, a mode now universally disused, if we except the Anabaptists, who are not very numerous. The change from immersion to infusion, was made in order to render the rite less disagreeable or dangerous. Protestants have carried the alteration still farther by way of improvement, and think it sufficient to administer it by aspersion. Thus it appears that the apostolic mode is rejected nearly by the consent of all parties; and, what is remarkable, that Protestants, quite contrary to the spirit of Protestantism, are farthest of all removed from it.

The Roman ritual supposes that the unbaptized infant is the temple of Satan for the moment, or the habitation of the devil. Accordingly, repeated exorcisms are used for the timely removal of the evil spirit, and he is peremptorily ordered by the exorcist to quit his strong hold as a necessary preliminary to the leading part of the baptismal ceremony. These exorcisms suppose the existence of original sin in its most frightful shape ; and are indeed so terrific altogether that they are never read like other portions of the ritual in the vernacular language. In fact, these same exorcisms are not fit for public ears, and therefore are not translated. And if so, what remains to be done but to condemn their introduction and their use, to expunge them altogether from the ritual, and to new model or to purify the administration of this initiatory rite.

When this portion of the ceremony was first introduced and established, no doubt the common doctrine respecting the state of new born infants was in full accordance with it, namely, that original sin placed them completely in the power of the devil; for the exorcisms in question necessarily imply this doctrine. However, though the exorcisms are still continued, in compliance, we should think, with established customs, the implied doctrine appears to have undergone a great alteration. It is now believed that the devil has not all that extraordinary power over unbaptized infants; who if they die in that state, instead of being condemned to eternal torments, as Augustine believed, are doomed to suffer no pain whatever, save the pain of loss, that is, exclusion from the bliss of heaven; a doctrine harsh enough in all conscience, and which very gratuitously, yet compassionately, establishes a fourth place in the invisible world. How complicated has religion become through the wild theories of adventurous theologians!! Was baptism ever administered without these infernal exorcisms? And how long will such hideous language disgrace the Roman ritual? We may venture to answer the former question in the affirmative; but to determine the latter would require the spirit of prophecy.

And why not expunge them at once, particularly as they are admitted to have no reference to the validity of the rite; and accommodate the church ceremonial to the alteration in church doctrine? But there are other exorcisms that should share the same fate—very many—exorcisms of things animate and inanimate—occupying a large portion of the Roman ritual, and all of a piece; all indeed so many charms for expelling devils or counteracting their malignant influence. This sweeping retrenchment is demanded by religion, at the expense of church unity; which indeed was infringed by their first introduction, as it must be at one time or other again by their abolition.

Confirmation as well as baptism is a drawback on church unity. It is administered in the eastern churches as in the Protestant, without consecrated oil; neither does its administration always come from the hands of a bishop. Here the Greeks differ in two important particulars from the Latins, but not at all from the primitive practice of the church. In the first ages we find little mention of consecrated oils, which now compose the great materiel of religion ; and we learn from St. Jerome, that, even in his time, bishops, with the exception of holy orders, shared with the inferior clergy the administration of all the rites of religion.

In the primitive church confirmation immediately followed baptism, to which it was considered a sort of supplement. A different view seems to be taken of it at present, at least in old Ireland ; for confession or penance, and the Eucharist or Lord's Supper, must be previously received by way of preparation ; so that instead of holding the second place, as in times past, or coming immediately after baptism, it should be now number four in the sacramental catalogue. Its position as to use or administration is quite altered. It is removed to a distance from baptism, perhaps not without cause. For it would not comport well with the dignity of a bishop to be the ordinary minister of a mere supplementary rite. But these changes are accidental or unimportant. Be it so: let us go on.

From the altered shape the sacraments have assumed many theologians have maintained, that the church has a specific power over their matter and form, that is, to use the language of the schools, over their constituent elements. This extraordinary privilege, however, is not admitted to extend to baptism or the eucharist; whose matter and form respectively, the Gospel has very accurately defined; and which, consequently, by the admission of all, have been specifically instituted by Jesus Christ. The other five, which, strictly speaking, are not considered sacraments by Protestants, seem to have been committed for their finish or perfection, to the regulation of the church; which, in the plenitude of her authority has, accordingly, determined the various forms for their administration respectively. It is therefore by no means unorthodox to suppose, that the church has specified the matter and form of confirmation, penance, extreme unction, holy orders and matrimony; and therefore, that Jesus Christ did not institute these rites in the same absolute unqualified manner as he did the sacrament of baptism and the Lord's Supper. This is not far from Protestantism.

This question of matter and form leads to considerable discrepancies in religion. The forms of the eastern church do not agree with the forms of the western. In the east the form of absolution is deprecatory; in the west it is absolute; or, to speak more intelligibly, the Greek priest beseeches the Almighty to grant pardon to the penitent sinner, whereas the Latin priest boldly grants pardon in his own name. It appears that the matter of this sacrament has not even yet been fully determined—some making it to consist in the extension of the minister's hand over the penitent; others in the acts of the penitent—contrition, confession and satisfaction. The fathers of Trent call these acts the "*quasi materia sacramenti*," the probable, or in some sort the matter of the sacrament; without telling us however, what is the "*vera et genuina materia*"—the true and genuine matter. Thus it appears that the constituent elements of penance are still floating on the waves of uncertainty.

There is no sacrament that labours under so many doubts and difficulties, as to matter and form and other points likewise as that of matrimony. Some say the form is pronounced by the officiating minister; others by the parties themselves; who, it is said, supply both matter and form; and, being thus at once both administrators and receivers, leaves to the priest nothing but the sorry office of witnessing the transaction. Previous to the Council of Trent, marriages contracted without the presence of the priest were considered valid; but since that period are pronounced null and void. This is a serious alteration—a break in upon unity—affecting the very vitality of a sacrament. Further, if the contracting parties be the ministers of this sacrament, it follows that priests cannot have the administration of it, unless, like the priests of the east, and the reformed clergy, they themselves enter into the holy bonds of matrimony; which unfortunately they are precluded from doing by the discipline of celibacy.

Matrimony has undergone changes without number, since the first establishment of the church. It is held at present by the church of Rome to be indissoluble. This was not the case in former times. Divorces on the score of adultery were common in many churches in the early ages. This discipline continued without interruption in the eastern church, and remains in force to this day. In the west the contrary discipline finally prevailed; though many instances could be produced of marriages having been dissolved even without the plea of adultery. In fact, the question of matrimonial indissolubility is not yet fully determined. The canon of the Council of Trent, on the subject, is equivocal; and was drawn up on purpose in that manner, at the instance of the Venetian ambassadors, to avoid giving offence to the Greek subjects of that republic. This was to sanction diversity instead of unity; and, out of human compliment, or through human respect, to make the Spirit blow hot and cold.

In the early ages, with some churches, second marriages were disapproved of, and third marriages were absolutely prohibited as unlawful. At the present day, there are no limits in this respect. But if the present system be lax one way, it is extremely strict in another. Persons in holy orders are excluded from the benefits and graces of this sacrament; and this by way of rendering them more perfect. The Roman Catholic church honours matrimony, and undervalues it at the same time. It is allowed to be a sacrament, and, consequently, a channel of divine grace; and yet, by clerical celibacy, it is pronounced to be a drawback upon sanctity. This is a sort of contradiction. But there is also another inconsistency in this matter. It is the reception of holy orders that begets the disqualification for matrimony. Holy orders, therefore, and matrimony—two sacraments—are placed in opposition to one another. The church, at its outset, knew nothing of all these anomalies; and the great eastern division still rejects them. As to the reformed, they stick to the letter of the Scripture, which is plain enough on the subject.

In the first centuries, we find little or nothing said of extreme unction, a very unaccountable thing, if we suppose that it was then administered as it is now. This shows that the primitive church did not attach the same import to the words of St. James, respecting this matter, that we do now-a-days. It would appear also, from church history, that the lower classes did not always receive the benefits of this sacrament. The Waldenses or Vadois, a sect that sprung up in the thirteenth century, reject it, because they said it was administered only to the wealthy; so that this portion of religion, it may be said, has undergone a variety of changes. First, it remained for a long time in a state of suspension; secondly, it was confined to the rich or higher orders; and lastly, it was administered indiscriminately to all classes, which is the present impartial discipline. For if it be beneficial, why should any class be shut out from its benefits? We might put a similar question respecting matrimony. But let us proceed to ring more changes on the subject of religion to the great prejudice of church unity.

It was formerly accounted not only lawful, but meritorious, to persecute heretics or persons dissenting from established orthodoxy, even unto death. This is an ancient error. Christianity, which had been persecuted by Paganism, retaliated with the utmost severity when it became itself triumphant. And when, through the obstinacy of some, and the unreasonableness of others, it was broken up into sects, the various classes or divisions thought themselves in duty bound to persecute one another. This error was therefore universal. In the time of the Reformation, a number of canons were framed at various councils, ordering bishops to search diligently in their respective diocesses after concealed heretics, and to have them delivered up to the secular arm. No Catholic in former times would dare preach the doctrine now so popular, of civil and religious liberty.

"They preach indeed, but practise not."

We are at liberty, however, to argue from their professions. Here, then, we find, that the Roman Catholic church has altered her doctrine in a matter that involves the rights and happiness of the human race ; and, what is very extraordinary, it was universally believed formerly, that this utter disregard for the rights of man, had the full sanction of the sacred writings. This was an error in morals, as it affected human rights, and an error in religion, as it involved a wrong interpretation of Scripture.

In this country, not many years ago, legal interest was condemned, as contrary to justice and to the gospel ; and the rule was, to refuse sacraments to all such as lent out money upon such conditions. Pawnbrokers, too, were ranked in the same class. This is not the case at present. It is no longer considered contrary to justice or the gospel, for a man to lend money on interest, or to follow the business of a pawnbroker. It is remarkable that Cloyne adhered to the old doctrine longer than Cork ; so that, for a considerable time, what was deemed agreeable to justice, in the latter diocese, was accounted a breach of it in the former.

As to astronomy or the system of the world, the church was formerly in the grossest ignorance. The system of Ptolomy, which makes the earth immoveable and the centre of motion for all the celestial bodies, was intimately blended with orthodoxy, and continued so until after the times of Copernicus and Galileo, both which philosophers had well nigh incurred the brand of heresy for having broached or revived the system now universally received. The Holy Fathers imagined that the earth was formed like a trencher, Jerusalem, the holy city, lying in the centre; somewhat like the ancient poets, who imagined that Delos, the birth-place of Diana and Apollo, occupied the middle point of the earth's surface—which question had been thus determined :

Jupiter let fly two eagles, one from the western extremity of the earth, the other from the eastern, which, steering their flight directly towards one another, with equal speed, met at length in the Island of Delos.

We should have taken no notice of this error, but that it was blended very preposterously with religion, and produced from time to time, many religious extravagancies. Virgilius, Bishop of Salzburg, long before the time of Copernicus and Galileo, was condemned for saying there were antipodes. In short, the church understood literally the words of Joshua, "Thou sun in the valley of Gibeon stand still;" and thus, notwithstanding her peculiar privilege of interpretation, entirely misunderstood that passage of the Scripture. But the church has altered her opinion on this as well as upon other matters, and no longer recognizes the system of Ptolomy, as part of orthodoxy. But how does all this square with her unity?

Magic, which is now universally exploded, formerly obtained universal credence. Thomas Aquinas and all the old schoolmen—the oracles of theology—have written copiously "*de maleficiis*" of witchcraft, and of the counteracting remedies. Our criminal code still contains laws—a dead letter to be sure—against such practices. Neither church or state had any doubt as to its reality. This is not the case at present. The church has become more enlightened, and laughs to scorn the absurd pretensions of witches, magicians, and necromancers.

This change is for the better; but we should suppose there was a change first of all for the worse; unless we take it for granted, that the mania of magic infested even the primitive churches—an admission which no Christian should make. Here, then, is change upon change, and that, too, regarding a matter of supernatural import. This is a strange kind of unity.

It must be admitted also that the church in former times was greatly in error respecting slavery and arbitrary domination. Exercising herself unbounded despotism, she fully sanctioned a similar system in the civil government. This is the reason why popery and slavery were usually coupled together. The canon law fully recognised the degrading condition of slavery; for servitude was numbered among the annulling impediments of matrimony; and it admitted, by adopting the rule "*partus sequitur ventrem*—the infant goes with the mother," that this inhuman degradation descended from the parent to the child as a melancholy inheritance. These doctrines are now loudly rejected by our sticklers for civil and religious liberty. Thus we find in the ages gone by a constant ebb and flow of doctrines touching morals, philosophy, politics, and religion. One word more and we shall conclude this chapter. Religious creeds have been constantly increasing in size and dimensions. The creed called the apostles' is the oldest and the shortest. The Nicene creed, which received several successive additions in the second and third councils of Constantinople, is much larger than that of the apostles. The creed attributed to Athanasius is still larger than that of Nice; and if the multiplied definitions "*de fide*" of the Council of Trent were congregated into one mass or body, a creed would be formed ten times larger than all the foregoing creeds put together. All this savours strongly of changes and alterations, additions and improvements. If it be said that church unity is to be referred only to the leading truths of Christianity, then the principle of Protestantism is admitted, and the groundless assumption of the Roman Catholic church in this respect has no other tendency than to confirm delusion and give stability to error.

CHAPTER XII.

OF TRANSUBSTANTIATION.

BOTH churches agree in admitting that the eucharist, or Lord's supper, is a sacrament of the first order; that it is the sacrament of the body and blood of Christ; that through the medium of the consecrated elements the body and blood of Christ are verily and indeed given to and received by the faithful; that it is a great blessing to receive it worthily, and a great misfortune to receive it unworthily. Both agree also in the general intention of adhering to the spirit of the original institution. It would be easy to shew, if both parties rested here, that all the ends of religion would be obtained as far as the sacrament is concerned. But this is out of the question. Such simplicity of doctrine would not give content to the pugnacious disposition of metaphysical polemics. It was deemed necessary to ascertain the exact nature of Christ's presence in the sacrament, and also how the elements of bread and wine are affected by consecration. Dupin and the Sorbonne, in their correspondence with Archbishop Wake, consented to give up Transubstantiation, or to expunge that objectionable term from the vocabulary of religion.

The church of England affirms that the natural body of Jesus Christ, with which, after his resurrection, he ascended into heaven, remains there; and consequently that its presence in the sacrament can only be figurative; and further, that the consecration of the sacred elements makes no change or alteration in their nature, though it elevates them to the dignity of a sacrament. On the other hand, Roman orthodoxy maintains, that the same natural body of Jesus Christ, which is in heaven and seated at the right hand of God, is really present in the sacrament; and also, that by the words of consecration, the *substance* of the bread is changed into Christ's body, and the *substance* of the wine into Christ's blood. It is, however, admitted, that his natural body is not present in a *natural manner*, but, as theologians express it, "*modo sacramentale*," "in a sacramental manner;" that his body is in heaven in its natural state, and in the sacrament *in a sacramental state;* that is, in a state or mode which cannot be defined nor apprehended. Quere—How does this differ from a figurative presence? Further, as to the change of the elements, it is not said simply, that the bread becomes the body, or the wine the blood of Jesus Christ, but that the *substance* of the bread is changed into the body, and the *substance* of the wine into the blood? Here comes the metaphysical theology. Let us endeavour to explain and explode it.

According to Aristotle and the schoolmen, body or matter consists of two properties—namely, *substance* and *accidents*, or accidental qualities. These qualities fall under the cognizance of the senses, and are called accidental, because, though generally essential to matter, they are not so specifically or individually. For example, wax may be soft or hard, may be moulded into this shape or that, may put on new forms and appearances without ceasing, however, through all these changes, to be wax. No particular form is essential to it, though it must, of necessity, appear under some form or other. So much for accidental qualities. We come now to *substance*, which is defined to be an essential attribute of matter, and the *substratum* or *subject*, in which the accidental qualities inhere. This essential attribute or property of matter does not fall under the cognizance of the senses, is invisible and impalpable, and only to be apprehended by the imagination. In short, though it is called an essential property of matter, it has nothing material in it, and should either be considered spiritual, which would be absurd, or a complete *non-entity;* so that the individual material substance or body is composed of all that and of nothing else but that, which falls under the cognizance of the senses. Substance, therefore, in matter or body, as contradistinguished from accidental qualities, according to Aristotle and the schoolmen, is no reality, but a mere figment of the imagination. Let us apply this reasoning to the question in hand. The change effected by the words of consecration does not, it is granted, affect the sensible or accidental qualities— the taste, the colour, the strength, the appearances. No alteration or metamorphosis takes place in this respect. The bread retains its nourishing, the wine its inebriating quality. This is granted; this must be granted. Even Thomas of Aquin says, that the senses are not deceived, because they pronounce judgment only on the accidental qualities, which of right fall under their cognizance. On what, therefore, does the power of transformation exert itself? On the imaginary attribute *substance*, which, contrary to the definition given of a noun substantive, can neither be seen, nor felt, nor heard, nor understood. What then shall we say of the doctrine of Transubstantiation? But that resting as it does upon an airy nothing, it must, "like the baseless fabric of a vision, disappear, and leave not a wreck behind." Transubstantiation, then, may be defined a transmutation of nothing; and we can arrive at no other conclusion but that all the churches of Christendom have been turned topsy-turvy on the subject, by absurd metaphysics and imaginary metamorphosis.

Further, it is admitted that the change or metamorphosis, real or imaginary, as the case may be, wrought by the all-powerful words of consecration, is but of a transitory nature. For when the elements begin to corrupt or suffer decomposition, the *substance*, which was supposed to have undergone the transformation, returns to its old state or relation, while the body of Christ withdraws from the decaying elements, or by the regular process of nature is re-transformed into the *substance* of the bread. Here is transmutation upon transmutation; or, more properly speaking, one absurdity generated by another.

Many Roman Catholic theologians are not afraid to advance opinions on this subject, that do not exactly tally with the definition given by the Council of Trent. They maintain that there is no conversion of one *substance* into another; but that, one is annihilated, and the other instantaneously substituted. Whether they believe a similar *vice versa* process takes place on the decay of the elements, does not appear. But to be consistent, they should believe so ; and that Christ's body is annihilated to make room for the reproduction of the bread. If this be not a *reductio ad absurdum*, there is nothing of the kind in Euclid.

Many theologians of all parties were of opinion that the question of Transubstantiation merely regards the mode or manner of Christ's presence in the sacrament, and therefore should be an open one, and not subjected to too severe a scrutiny. This, undoubtedly, was the opinion of Erasmus. Many of the Gallican doctors were willing to give way to the Calvinists in this point ; and the Lutherans were universally allowed to approach the confines of eucharistic orthodoxy. Is it possible, after all the wranglings, and disputations, and definitions, and anathemas, regarding an imaginary attribute of matter, *substance*, that all parties, casting aside the unintelligible jargon of the old school, will at length come to an agreement, and rest upon the common admission, that the body and blood of Christ, according to the simple words of the institution, are communicated to the faithful in the eucharist or Lord's Supper ?

The truth is, that the Lord's Supper, as to its contents, is a matter of observance rather than belief. It is a Christian institution, a monument of perpetual standing, the continued and universal celebration of which, is to remind Christian believers of the Victim slain on Mount Calvary, by the symbols of his body and blood, expressed in the consecrated elements, and given to the faithful. In this light was it considered by the Apostles and primitive Christians. In process of time it grew into the shape of a dogma, gradually swelled its consequence in the ranks of speculative tenets, until at length, in the revolution of times and principles, it was placed in the foreground of religion, and made the great standard of orthodoxy.

CHAPTER XIII.

OF THE MASS.

ROMAN Catholic orthodoxy is said to maintain that the celebration of the Lord's Supper, or of the eucharist, is a true and proper sacrifice offered to God for the living and the dead. This is denied by the reformers, who affirm that only one sacrifice, that of the cross, was offered up as the seal of the new covenant for the redemption of man. There appears to be here a wide difference between the parties at issue. But if the matter be properly examined, it will be found that the difference is not very extraordinary. Roman Catholic divines admit with the reformers, that there is but one individual sacrifice, namely, that of the cross ; with which they identify what is called the sacrifice of the mass. This theology, indeed, is not easily comprehended ; for, contrary to the laws of numbers, it confounds unity with multitude, and multitude with unity. They admit also, (for they must do so,) that no victim is slain on the occasion—that the shedding of blood, or the separation of the life-blood from the body, is merely figurative. This admission is tantamount to the figurative presence of the reformers. If the victim is slain only in figure, how can it be called a sacrifice in the true sense of the word? The sacrifice of the mass must be allowed, therefore, to labour under some sacrificial deficiency or imperfection. It wants absolutism or individuality, as it is identified with the sacrifice on Calvary ; and wants reality, as no victim is slaughtered. This cannot be said of the sacrifice of the cross, which is generally acknowledged to have been full, perfect, entire, complete. The question then comes to this, whether, under these circumstances, the Lord's Supper should be called a sacrifice ; in which case the dispute turns upon words. Bossuet does not urge this point far. After explaining, in a modest manner, the sacrificial qualities of the mass, and the figurative separation of the blood from the body of our Lord, he gives his opinion that the reformers should take no offence at its being called a sacrifice.

But let us examine the question as it is handled by those who call the mass, as they call the oblation on Calvary, the great sacrifice of the new law, and who are unwilling either to qualify or to concede. We must examine the matter critically. The celebration then of the eucharist, is considered a sacrifice, in the strict sense of the word. The act of celebration is, therefore, essentially different from the rite itself; for there is an essential difference between a sacrifice and a sacrament. But how can this be? How can the act of celebration be different from the rite itself, since it was by this same act that the sacrament was instituted? From this doctrine it would follow that Jesus Christ instituted a sacrament by the oblation of a sacrifice. This theology, whether well founded or not, is very complicated. There is in it a curious blending, an odd intermixture. The priest gives existence to the sacrifice, or he offers it; the sacrifice creates the sacrament; then, a sacrifice and a sacrament—two separate things—are coexistent in the same individual substance!!!!

The author of the epistle to the Hebrews institutes a comparison between the old law and the new, in respect to sacrifices; and he expressly says, that Christ Jesus, our high priest, offered himself but once. He speaks of the full, adequate, comprehensive efficacy of this sacrifice to the exclusion of every other. If the celebration of the eucharist was the great sacrifice of the new law, to be offered as such every where and at all times, from the rising to the setting sun, is it not passing strange that it was not noticed by him, more especially as he was writing expressly on the subject of sacrifices ? This argument, though a negative, is, from circumstances, equivalent to a positive, and cannot be easily got over.

Let us examine the matter a little farther. It is said, that the sacrifice of the mass is the same with the sacrifice of the cross; and that the merits of the latter are applied by the oblation of the former; that is to say, the application of merits is the same with the cause, by which these merits were produced. This explication or admission establishes not an identity but a diversity. The generative cause of a remedy must be different from the act of its application; unless the system of Spinoza be adopted, who identified or confounded all things—maintaining, that there is but one individual substance in the universe.

It must be granted that the eucharistic sacrifice is the same with that which Jesus Christ performed, when he instituted the eucharistic sacrament. If so much be conceded, a further concession must also be made, namely, that the effect then as well as now, was the application of the merits of the Saviour's sacrifice on the cross. Then it must be said that the merits of the latter sacrifice had been applied before the sacrifice itself took place. This is passing strange. It is turning things topsy turvy. It is not easy to conceive how the merits of Christ's death were applied before that event took place.

But supposing that the sacrifice offered by Christ at his Last Supper was the same with the sacrifice he offered shortly after on the cross, what must follow? If the former and the latter were one and the same oblation, one and the same individual sacrifice, it follows, that mankind were redeemed before Christ died on the cross; and that he yielded himself up a victim without necessity. See what a mass of difficulties besets that doctrine, which, departing from the simplicity of the original institution, gives to the Lord's Supper a complicated, inexplicable character.

A word as to the use made of this real or imaginary sacrifice. Masses are offered for a variety of purposes, at least in the minds of the multitude—for brute beasts as well as for human beings. A farmer, who happens to have his cattle disordered, the rot among his sheep, or the murrain among his cows, will have masses said for their recovery. The fishermen of Dungarvan, and elsewhere, regularly get masses said that they may hook the more fish. It is quite common among the ignorant to be under the persuasion that worldly calamities result from the agency of evil spirits; which opinion, indeed, receives some countenance from the book of Job. To counteract this malignant influence, they fly to the priest to have masses said. The priest takes no pains to remove the error, but accepts the pecuniary offering. Friars carry this matter to the last extremity. There is a general impression, as we have said elsewhere, that the masses of friars are more efficacious than those of the secular clergy. This impression answers the intended purpose ; it brings more money into the coffers of the friars, who, however, are not at a loss to assign a theological reason for the superexcellence of their masses—namely, that their state of life is more perfect than that of seculars—rather a knotty point to establish—as they make vows of poverty ; at the same time that, like Dives in the gospel, they are clothed in purple and fine linen, and fare sumptuously every day. The friars drive a considerable trade in masses. If a habit is to be blessed or consecrated, money must be given for masses, in order, of course, to ensure full efficacy to the benediction. These consecrated habits are supposed to be worn in the other world. It would be accounted a great misfortune for a poor person, residing in the neighbourhood of a friar to die without one. The blessing of the scapular, of which more hereafter, must have the same accompaniment as the blessing of the habit; and the ceremony of induction, or reception, or enrolment among the various confraternities and sisterhoods of Carmelites, of St. Francis, of St. Augustine and St. Dominick, ever superinduces a grateful commission for saying masses, which are offered up at once for the benefit of the individuals contributing, and for the confraternities at large, of which they then become members. This they call the communion of saints. The friar is the certain gainer in all these pious transactions.

The doctrine of purgatory has an intimate connection with the traffic in masses, which, in the church language, are offered up for the quick and for the dead. The piety of the living seeks to mitigate the sufferings of their departed friends. This piety is carefully nurtured by the interested clergy. The feast of all souls, or the beginning of November, as we have said elsewhere, is the critical period for the performance of this neighbourly and philanthropic duty. Nothing then is left untried to interest the faithful in behalf of the suffering souls in purgatory, who, it is said, can be most efficaciously relieved or extricated altogether, by the aid of masses, which are at once impetratory, propitiatory, and expiatory. This is a portion of the second of November doctrine, and which is inculcated by every means that avaricious ingenuity can devise. Money was formerly raised by the sale of indulgences, and it used to be said, that the deposit of the money in the holy box, or on the holy plate, suddenly threw open the gates of purgatory for the enlargement or escape of the poor suffering inmates. It was this and other ridiculous doctrines that first provoked the zeal of Luther, and prepared the way for the Reformation. Substitute for the old indulgences masses for the dead, and you have the same solemn farce acted over again. So much for the theory and practice of masses.

CHAPTER XIV.

In order to treat fully the subject in hand, that is, on a broad comprehensive scale, we think it right to take a cursory glance at the history of the church. It is a melancholy consideration, that at all periods, among those who professed to follow the same Gospel, were to be found persons, who, for trifling causes, were ever ready to involve the Christian community in rancorous disputes on religion. Under the old law matters were managed differently; a latitude was admitted in this respect, which in their present mood would give Christians great offence. The Sadducees did not believe in the immortality of the soul; and yet they worshipped in the synagogues, and offered sacrifices in the temple. It would appear from this, that the great test of orthodoxy among the Jews was the belief in one supreme being, the great creator of all things, who was, of course, to be reverenced, worshipped and obeyed.

The first converts to Christianity were Jews and Christians at the same time; nor, until the gospel had made considerable progress among the Gentiles, did it begin to be considered necessary to neglect or set aside the sacrifices and ceremonies of the Levitical law. The Christian ritual retains even still a portion of the Jewish ceremonial—the purification of women after child-birth. Thus it appears that apostolic Christianity, which ought, we should suppose, to be our model, did by no means include that principle of exclusiveness, which, it has been generally supposed, is one of the essential characteristics of orthodoxy. We may well cite here the words of Peter, addressed to Cornelius the centurion, and his family, when, by the direction of the Holy Spirit, he announced to them the glad tidings of the gospel: "Of a truth," said the Apostle, "I perceive that God is no respecter of persons, but in every nation he that feareth Him and worketh righteousness, is accepted with Him." This remarkable observation must have been referred to the religious position in which Cornelius stood previous to the commission that was given to Peter, of shedding in his house the light of the gospel. It appears, indeed, from the words of St. Luke in the same chapter of the Acts, that Cornelius had been always a favourite of heaven. "He was," said he, "a devout man, and one that feared God, with all his house, gave much alms, and prayed to God always." All this is at variance with the contracted views of modern orthodoxy, and should make us cautious how we limit the operation of God's goodness and mercy.

The creed, which is called after the Apostles, but was compiled in times subsequent, affords an instructive lesson on this subject. This short and simple compilation was put forth as the test of orthodoxy among the Christians of the first ages. It makes no reference, is indeed altogether silent, as to those points of doctrine and discipline, which, in after ages, and up to the present times, have distracted and divided the Christian world. If this comprehensive creed had maintained its original position, and continued as at first, to be deemed a sufficient test of orthodoxy, the church would, in all likelihood, have ever enjoyed tranquillity and peace.

This symbol may be said to be common to all Christian sects. It makes part of the Reformed as well as the Roman Catholic liturgy; is adopted in the east as well as in the west; is considered even by the church of Rome as a sufficient standard of faith for the reception of baptism or for admission into the church; and, if we except the Quakers, who are but a scanty flock, and the Presbyterians, who are indeed more numerous, and who reject it because it is not founded, *totidem verbis*, in the New Testament, it is the common and undisputed creed of all Christendom.

Here is a great rallying point for the union of the many sects, into which the great aggregate body of Christians is unhappily divided. This most ancient of all Christian creeds, compiled, if not by the apostles, certainly by apostolic men, from a due consideration of the nature and essence of the new covenant, says not a word about transubstantiation, nor consubstantiation, nor impanation; is silent as to *homoousion*, or *homoiousion;* defines nothing as to the plurality of Christ's nature or his will, or the individuality of his person; makes no reference to image worship, or to the propriety of praying to the saints, or to a world of other matters, that have furnished grounds for schisms, anathemas and excommunications. Is it possible that all this abstruse theology was unknown or overlooked at the time—that is, in the apostolic age, when the church was in its most perfect state, just formed by the hands of divine power and wisdom, innocent like our first parents in the garden of Eden, fresh, pure, and undefiled? If we take our stand upon this creed, we shall find that the benefits of Christianity may be accorded to all such as believe in God the Father, the creator of all things—in Jesus Christ his only Son, who became man through the operation of the Divine Spirit, triumphed over death and hell, ascended into Heaven, whence he will come again at the final resurrection, to judge all mankind and determine their everlasting doom in the world to come.

CHAPTER XV.

The Nicene creed, which was framed in the fourth century, contains much more than that of the Apostles. This creed, in its present form, is not, as a whole, the compilation of the Nicene fathers, to whose doctrinal dogmata, respecting the nature and dignity of the Son of God, additions were made respecting the Holy Ghost, or the third person of the Trinity, by councils subsequently held in Constantinople; and, finally, in the course of time, the words "*filio que*" were inserted by the western or Latin church. The Greeks, properly speaking, have never consented to this last addition or insertion. This creed gave occasion to mighty quarrels in theology. It branded with the mark of heresy the doctrine of Arius, who held, that the Son of God, the second person of the Trinity, should not be placed on a complete equality with the eternal Father. The Arians did not dispute the truth or the authority of anything contained in the Apostles' Creed, or the sacred writings. They deferred also to the recorded opinions of the ecclesiastical writers of the first three centuries, or of the fathers of the church, who had lived previous to their own times. They argued from Scripture and tradition; and from both these sources they thought themselves warranted in maintaining, that the doctrine of the consubstantiality of the Son with the eternal Father, was an innovation on primitive Christianity.

It was this term "consubstantial" or "*homo-ousion*" that furnished the great matter for disputation. The Arians objected to it altogether; while there appeared a want of uniformity and steadiness on the side of those who adopted it. It was not understood in the same sense by all the Nicene fathers, some maintaining that it did not imply an exact equality between the Father and the Son. This was in some sort to approve the doctrine of Arius, and to condemn it at the same time. There is no doubt also that the fathers, who lived before that time, have many passages in their writings expressive of the inferiority of the Son; and it is a curious fact that most of the leading bishops who sided Arius in this controversy, were the scholars of Lucian, a celebrated priest of Antioch, who had suffered martyrdom in the persecution of Dioclesian, and was considered one of the most learned and most sanctified men of his time.

The decision of Nice also appeared contradictory to that of a council held at Antioch, about sixty years previous, where, in pronouncing condemnation on the doctrine of Paulus Samosatenus, who said, that Christ was a mere man, they rejected the term "*homoousion*," as being inapplicable to the Son of God. No doubt the Arians believed their own doctrine to be in conformity with the decision of this council.

Further, Hosius, Bishop of Corduba, or Cordova, who presided at the Council of Nice, and who was called the father of the councils, from having presided over so many—a man held in the utmost esteem and veneration—towards the latter part of life, signed a confession of faith that did not include this much-disputed term. It is also said that one of the reasons why the term itself was adopted, was, because it was put forward by the Arians as a negative—that is, as an adjunct not applicable to the Son of God; relying, probably, on the decision of the Council of Antioch, already mentioned. The term thus introduced was laid hold on for the more effectual and more pointed condemnation of Arius. Some of the ancient fathers make it a matter of triumph, that the Arians themselves furnished the weapon for their own destruction. St. Ambrose says, Lib. 3, cap. *ult de fide*, "*Hoc verbum posuere Patres quod viderunt adversariis esse formidini; ut tanquam evaginato ab ipsis gladio, ipsum nefandæ caput heresios amputarent.*" The fathers put forward this term, of which they saw the others (the Arians) had a horror; so that it may be said the head of their impious heresy was amputated with the very sword which they themselves had unsheathed. The adoption of the term may be justifiable, but the motive for doing so was otherwise, if we may credit Ambrose.

The Arians objected to nothing in the creed, save the term "*homoousion*, or consubstantial." They were perfectly satisfied with the expression "begotten of the Father and born before all ages," or all worlds, "God of God," "Light of Light." It may be here remarked, that some of the church formularies, even of the present day, do not seem to imply, in regard to the Son, an absolute or perfect equality with the Father. For example—the "*Te Deum.*" This hymn, which makes part of the *reformed* as well as the Roman liturgy, characterizes the Son very differently from the Father. "The Father, (it says,) of *immense majesty.*" "*Patrem immensæ majestatis.*" But of the Son it says, "*venerandum tuum verum et unicum filium.*" Thy venerable and only Son. An Arian would have no difficulty in chanting this hymn conjointly with the orthodox.

We do not here advocate Arianism, but we are endeavouring to shew that the professors of that doctrine, who, in the early ages, were very numerous and very influential, did not merit unqualified condemnation. The subject is not well understood; let us pursue it a little farther.

Arianism and orthodoxy were for a considerable time blended together. All parties were accustomed indiscriminately to assemble in the same church. If we except the doxology and trisagion, which began to be in use after the Council of Nice, the liturgy, or the mode of celebrating the divine worship, was the same with both. Arian and orthodox bishops used to occupy the same see alternately.

They all believed in the same one, eternal, supreme God—the Lord and Maker of all things; they all equally believed Jesus Christ to be the great mediator between God and man; and they all acknowledged with equal thankfulness the various and multiplied manifestations of the Holy Spirit. No missionaries were ever more zealous than Arian bishops and priests for the conversion of the idolaters. It was by their preaching and ministry that the Goths and Vandals—the idolatrous barbarians of the North—were converted to Christianity. And it was an Arian bishop who made the famous reply to the Emperor Julian, who, when passing through Antioch, on his route to the Persian war, where he lost his life, having asked him, in a tone of irony, how was the carpenter's son then employed—meaning Jesus Christ—received this bold and prophetic answer, "He is employed, (said this Arian bishop,) in making thy coffin." The disastrous result of the expedition established the truth and the point of the replication. It would be ungracious to say, that this bold advocate for Jesus Christ was excluded from the pale of Christianity; or that those zealous and indefatigable missionaries, who persuaded great and powerful nations to relinquish their idols and embrace the gospel, should, nevertheless, themselves be denied the benefit of Christian redemption.

It seemed a matter of course that the nature of the Divine Word being ascertained, an inquiry should also be set on foot respecting the nature or rank of the Holy Ghost—the third person of the Trinity. Accordingly, a great controversy arose upon this point. The divinity or deity of the Holy Ghost was maintained by some and denied by others; at the head of which latter was Macedonius, patriarch or bishop of Constantinople. Several councils or assemblies of the clergy were held on the subject in that great city, and the final result was, a doctrinal definition in favour of the divinity of the Holy Spirit. This definition, however, was drawn up with great caution. The Holy Ghost is not said, like the Son, to be true God of true God, or consubstantial to the Father. He is, however, defined to be the Lord and Giver of life, and is said to be adored and glorified together with the Father and the Son; and to have proceeded from the Father, which last characteristic is taken out of the New Testament.

It does not appear that the doctrine of the absolute deity of the Holy Spirit was universally received at that time. To prove this, it may be sufficient to cite Eusebius of Cæsarea, the great ecclesiastical historian, and the most learned man of his time. This celebrated writer was acquained with the works of all the fathers or ecclesiastical writers that preceded him, up to the times of the apostles. He has given us, in his ecclesiastical history of the three first centuries, passages or extracts from three hundred ecclesiastical writers, whose works are all lost, save and except what is preserved in this great compilation. This writer asserts, in his book of evangelical preparation, and in his third book of ecclesiastical history, "that the Holy Spirit is neither God nor the Son of God, because he does not derive his origin, like the Son, from the Father, (for he *proceeds* from the Father,) being (he says) of the number of those things that were made by the Son."

It may not be out of place also to quote this same father on the doctrine of consubstantiality. He acquiesced, after some hesitation, in the decision of the Nicene Council; but he gives an explanation of the term "*homoousion*," that does not place the Son of God upon a perfect equality with the Father. His words are found in an apologetic epistle, which he wrote to his own diocese, or church, immediately after signing the formulary of the council. "When it is affirmed, (says he,) that the Son is consubstantial to the Father, the meaning is only that the Son of God has no resemblance to any creature made by him, (the Son,) but a perfect resemblance to the Father, by whom he was begotten, and not by any other subsistence or substance." In his fourth book of evangelical preparation, he also says, "that the Son is not to be adored but on account of the Father, who dwelleth in him." In chapter the 8th, he says likewise, "The Son is a Lord inferior to the Father;" and again, he says, "The glory of the Son is less than the glory of the Father, and that the Son is not entitled to the same honour with the Father. Such is the language of Eusebius, bishop of Cæsarea—the great ecclesiastical historian and father of the church—respecting the second and third persons of the Trinity. Whether his doctrine can be made to square with that of Athanasius we shall not inquire; but one thing is certain, he was always reckoned an orthodox bishop and a holy man.

From all this it would appear that much misunderstanding existed on this subject; and it would seem to follow, that no outcry should be raised against those Christians who, in paying the tribute of divine worship, think it right to restrict themselves to the Father alone; in whom, to use the words of St. Paul, "all live and move and have their being." The Nicene bishops themselves only defined the consubstantiality of the Son, in as much as it was compatible with the unity of God; for they commenced their profession of faith not like the Apostles' creed with the simple words "I believe in God," but with the phrase "I believe in *one* God," thus specifying at the very outset their unqualified belief in the unity of the Godhead. Some Arians, perhaps, argued, that the doctrine of the *homo-ousion* implied a plurality of Gods, and transformed Christianity into polytheism. To rebut this charge, the Nicene fathers commenced, by professing their belief in "one God alone." This was a kind of salvo against the consequences deducible in the minds of some, from the doctrine they subsequently laid down respecting the nature and prerogatives of the Son of God. All classes, therefore, Arians and orthodox, were agreed in this one great fundamental dogma—that, under all circumstances, no matter what doctrine is to be held, respecting the sublime nature of the Son and the Holy Spirit, no tenet is or ought to be upheld at variance with the complete and absolute unity of the Godhead.

CHAPTER XVI.

The Nicene creed, besides receiving additions in the eastern or Greek church, received also a small augmentation in the western or Latin church. It was defined in the east agreeably to the words of Scripture that the Holy Spirit—the Paraclete—proceeds from the Father. The Latins in some subsequent age went farther, and determined that there was a sort of two-fold procession, namely, that the Holy Ghost proceeds from the Father and the Son. It is not ascertained at what precise time the Nicene creed received this enlargement; but whatever circumstances gave rise to its commencement, it became the adopted doctrine of the whole western church. If we may hazard a conjecture, one might say that the addition in question was a sort of corollary from the identification of the Son with the Father by the Nicene synod. However this may be, the Greeks, though they admitted the identification, would not subscribe to the corollary, and do still differ, or appear to differ, from the Latins on the subject. The terms *filioque*, or the corresponding terms in the Greek tongue, have never been inserted in their creed. This difference, indeed, appeared to have been adjusted at the Council of Florence, where, after a schism that had lasted for centuries, a temporary re-union took place between the rival churches. After much debate and altercation, both parties at length agreed, that the doctrines of the east and west, respecting the procession of the Holy Spirit, *when duly explained*, were not in reality different; that the Latins did not hold, as the Greeks imagined, the doctrine of a double procession, or deny that the Father was the source and principle of the Godhead. On the contrary, they held that there was but one single procession or spiration; so that the Holy Ghost proceeds from the two as from one principle. Thus, notwithstanding the inveteracy of the schism, when both parties met amicably together and entered coolly and dispassionately into the inquiry, it was found that they had all along misunderstood one another; and that if any doctrinal difference at all was in question, it was such as ought not to interrupt the harmony of the two churches.

CHAPTER XVII.

In the eastern church there are some sects or divisions; the chief of which are the Nestorians, the Eutichians, and the Monothelites. The errors or doctrines of these sectaries made a prodigious noise in the early ages of Christianity. After the definition of the Council of Nice, respecting the consubstantiality of the Son, the Virgin Mary began to be called the Mother of God. This appellation was very startling and extraordinary; but was justified as a necessary inference from the admitted Godhead or Deity of the Son. Nestorius, patriarch of Constantinople, a learned and eloquent prelate, considered the appellation impious and absurd; for, said he, as God had no mother, so no woman should be called the mother of God. She was, he said, the mother of Christ, the man God, and nothing more—agreeable to the words of the apostle "what is born of flesh is flesh." The zealots for this high-sounding epithet took great offence at these observations of Nestorius, and, turning the tables on the bishop, they proclaimed that he wished to divide Christ into two separate subsistences; as if the Son of God was one person and the man Christ another. Nestorius on the other hand accused them of confounding the two natures, the divine and human; of making the divine nature to be born of Mary, and converting the flesh of Jesus Christ into the Godhead. On this account, he said, they gave to the Mother of Christ the title of "Mother of God." This is what Nestorius himself says of the matter, in a justificatory epistle, which he wrote on the subject, to Pope Celestine. He admitted the union of two natures in Jesus Christ, but he affirmed that what was proper or peculiar to the divine nature could not be attributed to the human; nor, *vice versa*, what was proper to the human, be attributed to the divine; and therefore, that the Virgin Mary ought not to be entitled the "Mother of God." This reasoning of Nestorius is very plausible. However, it had no other effect at the time but to set the whole Christian world in commotion; and, finally, to subject himself, being first branded as a heresiarch, to perpetual exile and degradation.

The dread of inferences seems to have been the cause why the two parties were so positive in maintaining their respective opinions. Nestorius imagined that the appellation—Mother of God—involved the confusion of the two natures; whilst his opponents—the followers of Cyril—contended that the rejection of that extraordinary appellation disjoined the two natures altogether.—Properly speaking it was nothing more than a metaphysical dispute on an unintelligible subject, between persons who, in reality, were of the same doctrine. Such was the opinion entertained of the matter by Theodoret, John of Antioch, and many other celebrated men of the time.

CHAPTER XVIII.

Eutichianism sprung quite naturally from a spirit of opposition to Nestorianism. Eutiches and his followers, applying their reasoning faculties to a very dark subject, came to the conclusion that the Virgin Mary was entitled to the appellation of "Mother of God," because the two natures were, in reality, blended together from the moment of the incarnation. This, they contended, was the identical doctrine of St. Cyril, the great opponent of Nestorius; nor is there any doubt that this was the doctrine to which Nestorius was opposed. The Eutichians, too, persisted in their opinion, under the impression, that the complete separation of the two natures was the doctrine or error of Nestorius; and which, they fancied, had been condemned as heretical in the Council of Ephesus. It was, indeed, the dread of error, that caused both Nestorius and Eutiches to enact so extraordinary a part on the theatre of religion. Nestorius, to prevent the confusion of the two natures, used some expressions, which seemed to imply that the person of the Son of God was not identified with the person of Jesus Christ; whilst Eutiches, for fear of disturbing this same identity, appeared to confound both natures, each, however, denying the conclusions that were drawn from their expressions. The whole controversy turned upon disputed words and disputed inferences, on the propriety or impropriety of using this or that form of language. In short, three unintelligible terms, substance, person, and nature, as applied by them to Jesus Christ, set all the churches of Christendom in an uproar, and branded, as heresiarchs and imps of Satan men, who, if matters were duly sifted and weighed, would have been found neither opposed to one another, nor to the councils that condemned them. A number of bishops, whose orthodoxy was never impugned, were persuaded of the orthodoxy of Nestorius ; and the only fault they found with him was, that he persisted in his refusal to call Mary the Mother of God. Dioscorus of Alexandria, also, and a multitude of other bishops assembled at Ephesus, acquitted Eutiches. Yet one would imagine from all that was said and done on these occasions, the councils that were assembled, the battles of the bishops, the conflicting anathemas that were pronounced, the immensity of official correspondence that took place, the sermons that were preached, and the treatises that were written and circulated, that the very foundation of religion or the existence of the Deity was placed in jeopardy.

CHAPTER XIX.

The Monothelites, or those who affirm that there is but one will or moving power in Jesus Christ, form no inconsiderable sect in the eastern church. This doctrine, which was unheard of for so many centuries, began to be agitated about the year 620. Monothelitism originated with some of the leading bishops, was maintained by several successive patriarchs of Constantinople, and received at once the sanction of Honorius, the Roman Pontiff. This doctrine came very near that of the Monophysites, or the followers of Eutiches, (or, as they themselves say, of St. Cyril,) who confounded the two natures in Christ; and, if pronounced orthodox, might have been a means, provided all parties reasoned consequentially, of their re-union with the Catholic church. This object, indeed, was contemplated. The doctrine itself, however, met at once with opposition, and was finally rejected and condemned in the sixth general council as inconsistent with the doctrine of the two-fold nature defined against Eutiches in the Council of Chalcedon. Nor did the fathers rest satisfied with the condemnation of the doctrine. They anathematised, in their tombs, as heretics, the bishops who had maintained it—Cyrus of Alexandria, Sergius of Constantinople, several patriarchs who succeeded them, and even Honorius, the Roman pontiff, all of whom had

had the folly to imagine that their faith was orthodox, and who had died, to all appearance, and in the judgment of the faithful, true members of the Catholic church.

Whoever with an unbiassed mind will read the history of these transactions, the proceedings in council and the proceedings out of council, will see that the conclusions come to were the result of metaphysical reasoning; and that the definition of this third Council of Constantinople, against Monothelitism, gave the stamp of orthodoxy to a doctrine—that of a two-fold will in Christ—of which no trace can be discovered in the ages preceding.

Further, the anti-Monothelites admitted, that, between the two wills in question, no discrepancy did or could exist; which doctrine, considered under any and every point of view, is tantamount to the identity or amalgamation of the wills, agreeably to the doctrine of the Monothelites; so that the difference lay in expression rather than opinion, was verbal not real. It is indeed astonishing to see how the church was distracted by factions and divisions for so many centuries; all fighting, "*unguibus et dentibus*," tooth and nail, on subtle, unintelligible distinctions and expressions; raising new questions and giving doctrinal definitions on subjects, unheeded and unknown in the ages preceding—whereas, in the Christian religion, there should be nothing new or novel—and causing even orthodoxy itself to veer from side to side, according to the prevailing current of public opinion. For if we make a comparison or analysis of things and events, we must arrive at the conclusion, that the doctrine of Chalcedon agreed with that of Nestorius, and Monothelitism with that of Eutiches. Most certainly, if Nestorius had been alive at the time, and present at the council just mentioned, he would most willingly have subscribed to the doctrine put forth regarding the two natures; as he would also, in after times, to the doctrine of the two wills. Upon these two occasions, if he had been living, he would have been found to be orthodox, though he was called a second Judas, deposed, anathematized, and treated with the utmost indignity by the first Council of Ephesus. The only difference that may be supposed to exist between Nestorius and the fathers of these councils is, that they admitted the propriety of calling Mary the Mother of God—that is, though they maintained the distinction of the two natures, and the two wills—keeping the human separate from the divine—still they admitted that what was affirmed of one may be affirmed of the other—a communication of terms—and that the maternity of Mary, which could only regard the man, (Jesus Christ,) may also be applied to, or predicated of, the Incarnate Word. How small the difference! Nevertheless, Nestorius, as he happened unfortunately to be condemned by a council headed by St. Cyril, to whom the Monophysites look up as their patriarch, he continued, and still continues to be regarded as a heretic; and the sect that take their denomination from him, still forms a separate congregation, and are excluded from the privileges of orthodoxy.

How easily is schism engendered, and how difficult to effect a re-union! The stability of religion and the peace of the church seem to require, that general councils should be deemed infallible; and therefore, that their decisions are irreversible. But has this high prerogative—assumed as it is—produced the desired effect? Have the decisions of general councils produced peace in the church and unity in matters of religion? The history of the church, both eastern and western, replies in the negative. The reason is, that they have not kept themselves within proper boundaries, have defined things that are undefinable, and treated matters of opinion as undoubted matters of revelation.

The extraordinary title of Mother of God gave offence to Nestorius, who opposed it in such a manner that he seemed to separate the person of the Son of God from the person of the man Christ. This brought into the arena of controversy the defenders of the novelty complained of by Nestorius. These contended that the human person and the divine person in Jesus Christ were one and the same; and, therefore, that Mary, his Mother, may be called the Mother of God. This doctrine, which was incorporated with orthodoxy by the Synod of Ephesus, led to that of the confusion of the human nature with the divine, a doctrine which soon after took the name of Eutichianism. The confounding of the two natures was considered as trenching too much on the majesty of the Godhead, and it was defined accordingly that the two natures were separate and distinct in the one person, Jesus Christ. This was in some sort to blend together the respective doctrines of Nestorius and Eutiches. Then, after a considerable lapse of time, comes Monothelitism, which was a sort of corollary from the definition of the first Council of Ephesus, as to the identity of persons in Jesus Christ. The Monothelites contended that one individual person could not be supposed to have more than one will. This opinion, however, could not be reconciled with the definition of Chalcedon, respecting the separate existence of the natures; and, therefore, as the nature of Christ was two-fold, so also is his will; both natures and both wills being, however, intimately united. Thus we see how one doctrinal definition led to a series of others, each successive one arising from the preceding, and giving rise to the succeeding, being at once a consequence and a cause. Can any one say that this is not the mode of extending the boundaries of religion, of generating articles of faith, and of subverting the simplicity of the gospel?

CHAPTER XX.

THE fourth and fifth centuries are the most remarkable in the history of the church, for the holding of councils to determine doctrinal disputes. The Council of Nice was so far from allaying the controversy on the equality or inequality of the Son with the Father, that councils innumerable were subsequently held in the east and in the west on that abstruse subject. The doctrine of infallibility does not appear to have been well understood at that time. The term *consubstantial* or "*homo-ousion*" gave very general offence ; and bishops without number were of opinion that Arius was orthodox. A great number of new creeds, or formularies of belief, were drawn up at the various councils held in all quarters, in which the disputed "term" was omitted ; and even the tide of opinion ran so much in that direction, that Athanasius, the great opponent of Arius, was condemned. The bishops, to the number of ninety, assembled at Antioch in the year 341—that is, sixteen years after the time of the Nicene Synod—made a solemn declaration, that they thought it incumbent on them to restore Arius to the communion of the church ; because, upon due examination, they found his doctrine to be orthodox. They affirmed that they were not his followers, but that the doctrine they believed and professed, was that which was handed down to them. They also drew up a confession of faith, which is considered to be perfectly unobjectionable, save that it does not include the term "*consubstantial.*" If these bishops formed a correct opinion of Arius and his doctrine, and that his creed coincided with their's, it would seem that the fathers of Nice had been mistaken, and had condemned him unjustly.

In the year 359, a council, consisting of 400 bishops, from all the western provinces of the empire, was assembled at Arminium or Rimini, to re-examine the definition of the Nicene Synod respecting the consubstantiality of the Son of God. At the commencement of their sittings, they decided in favour of the Nicene creed, and refused to sanction the subsequent dissenting decisions of the eastern bishops on the subject. But they did not hold firm to this decision. They were induced to examine the question again *de novo*, when they rejected the term "*consubstantial,*" and expressed their concurrence in the anti-Nicene doctrine of the eastern bishops.

The same year a corresponding council was held at Seleucia, in the east; where, after some debates and controversy, it was at length finally determined that they should abide, not by the definition of the Nicene council, but by the profession of faith made at the Council of Antioch, already mentioned, where Arius was pronounced orthodox, and the term "*consubstantial*" omitted.

But this state of things did not continue. The tide of church opinion began again to flow in an opposite direction. The definition of Nice had its supporters, more especially (strange to say) in the west. The bishops of Arminium, when they returned to their respective churches, protested separately against the decision, which they, as a congregated body, had put forth to the world. In the east, after the death of Constantius, the Arians began to lose ground, and the doctrine of "*consubstantiality*" finally gained the ascendant.

CHAPTER XXI.

THE Council of Ephesus, which condemned Nestorius, and called him a second Judas, because he refused to Mary the title of "Mother of God," had as little success as the Council of Nice, in producing Christian peace and uniformity. The result was nothing but contradiction and division, misapprehension and misrepresentation. The decision against Nestorius was come to with all the heat and haste imaginable. St. Cyril, who presided, was his determined adversary; and, accordingly, he opened the council and persuaded the bishops to come to a decision without waiting the arrival of John of Antioch, and the other prelates of Asia Minor; all of whom, without a dissentient voice, not only protested against what had been done, but even pronounced an excommunication against St. Cyril and his associates, for having unjustly condemned Nestorius. Fifty-six bishops acted with John of Antioch upon this occasion; that is, above one third of the number that sided with Cyril; among which latter, it may be remarked, were fifty who came from Egypt in the train of the Alexandrian bishop—his own suffragans; besides that several of the remainder, who had reluctantly signed the act of condemnation, disapproved of the rapidity with which the business had been transacted; for the whole process was gone through in one day's sitting. Here was council against council, anathema against anathema; Nestorius condemned and acquitted at the same time, by bishops too, who are all now accounted orthodox. The immediate consequence of all this was endless controversies, scandals and schisms. The words of Gregory Nazianzen, relative to the councils of his time, may well be applied to the Council of Ephesus under St. Cyril. "He never," he said, "saw an assembly of bishops that had a happy conclusion—that instead of remedying the evil, they always increased it—that their obstinate disputes and the ambition of overcoming and domineering, completely warp their judgments; and thus it generally happens, that they whose duty it is to judge others, are actuated more by ill-will than by a desire of reclaiming and correcting. What in this case becomes of infallibility?

CHAPTER XXII.

THE proceedings of the bishops, in the affair of Eutiches, were of a similar description. This heresiarch, as he is called, was persuaded that the doctrine he professed was that of Cyril, the opponent of Nestorius. Whether those who raised the outcry against him believed so or not, it may not be easy to determine; but from the decision come to, at the first great assembly that sat on the question, he had every reason to be fortified in the opinion he maintained. This synod, which was held at Ephesus, and at which Dioscorus, the successor of St. Cyril in the great see of Alexandria, presided, approved of the confession of faith presented by Eutiches on the occasion, and acquitted him of the charge of heresy. Doubtless the creed of Dioscorus was the same with that of his predecessor, Cyril. He came also to the council, attended by a great number of Egyptian bishops, just as Cyril did to the former council held in the same city against Nestorius. It is probable, too, that several of those that attended Dioscorus had been present at the former synod. The decision, therefore, on this first trial of Eutiches by an assembly, it should be remarked, consisting of 150 bishops, congregated from various quarters, was tantamount to this—that his doctrine did not differ from that of St. Cyril, or of the first council of Ephesus, where that patriarch presided. It would appear from all this, that Eutiches should be identified or classed with the celebrated bishop of Alexandria; that if the former be branded as a heretic, so should the latter; and if the bishop be considered orthodox, so should the unfortunate Archimandrite. Let us pursue this idea of reconciling matters.

The Nestorian party, dissatisfied with the decision of the council under Dioscorus, had the address to have another great council called at Chalcedon to re-examine the affair of Eutiches. The re-examination accordingly took place, and the result was, that the decision of Ephesus, in favour of Eutiches, was annulled, and the unhappy man himself branded for ever (like Nestorius) as an incorrigible heresiarch. The decision, however, of the first council of Ephesus against Nestorius was left undisturbed; and, by consequence, the orthodoxy of St. Cyril. Here then, after all, we have a point of meeting for the adverse parties. St. Cyril agreed in doctrine with the first council of Ephesus. His creed was also approved of in the second council held in the same city, where, in like manner, the seal of approbation was set to the doctrine of Eutiches, as in no wise differing from that of the Egyptian patriarch. Finally, the Council of Chalcedon, made up as it was of opposite parties, though it condemned Eutiches and the second Ephesian synod, still embarked in the same vessel with Cyril and his anti-Nestorian associates. We, therefore, have Nestorians, Eutichians, and Catholics, notwithstanding all their rancour and dissensions, blended together and united by a hallowed link of undisputed orthodoxy. In short, Cyril, whose memory the church has consecrated, is the great point of union and identity for all the clashing disputants regarding the unity of person and plurality of natures in Jesus Christ. But let us come down again to our own times and to our own religious differences.

CHAPTER XXIII.

OF CEREMONIES.

Nothing can be more complicated than the Roman Catholic ceremonial. Simplicity, the original characteristic of Christianity, has been abandoned. The Roman pontifical, containing the various ceremonies to be performed by bishops, is a volume of considerable bulk, larger by far than the New Testament. Catholic divines admit that this pontifical contains a great quantity of superfluous matter, which, however, is not to be passed over, so long as it remains on the statute book. The Council of Trent has even gone so far as to anathematize all such as should presume, of their own private authority, to retrench or to alter any portion of it. Bishops themselves, much less the clergy of the second order, have no choice or jurisdiction in such things. This law, however, is sometimes disregarded by refractory individuals, who, pressed by time, or actuated by carelessness, or for other reasons best known to themselves, skip over many of the prescribed ceremonies, and hasten to the conclusion of their work.

The ceremonies of the mass, how multifarious. Genuflections and crosses without number; complicated movements; the quarter wheel, the semicircular, and the circular, as the case may require; the repeated shifting of the book from side to side, and the blaze of candles amid the glare of the meridian sun. Doubtless the generality of priests attach little importance to these matters; not so the congregation, who would be highly scandalized, if the mass suffered any defalcation in this respect.

The devotional exercises of the multitude in general, are of a very odd description; scarcely a house without a consecrated bead, a religious piece of furniture supposed to possess extraordinary virtue, particularly if consecrated by the Pope. This guides them in the arrangement of their prayers, most of which are addressed to the Blessed Virgin, whom the bead-gentry invoke ten times for once they invoke the Almighty. Nor is this mode of praying confined to the vulgar and illiterate. It is prescribed in the common prayer books, is repeated by priests publicly at the altar, and is practised in all the nunneries and religious communities. The costume of a nun is incomplete unless a consecrated bead hangs dangling from her girdle. In the chair of confession the satisfactory works imposed generally consist of so many rosaries to be repeated on the five decad or fifteen decad bead within a certain limited time. At the mass, especially in country chapels, you will scarcely hear any thing but rosaries—*Ave Maria* ten times, and *Pater Noster* once. This disproportionate alternation is kept up without intermission from the beginning to the end of mass, from the "*Introibo*," to the gospel of St. John. If they stay at home from mass on a Sunday or holiday, they repeat a rosary or two on their bead as a set-off against the omission. In short, the rosary, which should be called their devotion to the Virgin, forms the sum total of their religious worship. The Virgin is transformed into a divinity, of whom her female votaries constantly crave pardon for their transgressions. The Colliridiani, as we learn from Epiphanius, were condemned as idolaters in the primitive church, for a custom they observed, of offering a cake as a sort of sacrifice, in honour of the Virgin. It would not be easy to show that the cake of the Colliridiani was more opposed to the purity of divine worship than this perpetual rosary. It is, indeed, quite certain, that the Virgin never enjoyed higher honors or prerogatives than she does among her female votaries now-a-days, at least in old Ireland. The late Dr. Moylan, Roman Catholic bishop in Cork, ordered the litany of the Blessed Virgin, or the Litany of our Lady of Loretto, (a place celebrated in the annals of sacrilegious romance,) to be recited always before mass, throughout his diocess; which odd practice is still observed under his enlightened successor. He also instituted monthly processions, at which this litany is chanted in her honour.

The litany in question is nothing but a formidable series of adulatory epithets bestowed on the Virgin for the purpose of procuring her favour and intercession. It is of general use, and is reckoned by some indispensable. It is, however, more common in some places than in others, more used by women than by men, and more by the ignorant than by the well-informed. The priest recites the litany on his bended knees; but, when the mass commences, he stands erect. This is odd enough. He addresses the Virgin on his knees, and he addresses the Almighty in a standing posture. He shews more respect to the creature than to the Creator. Much the same happens when the hymn

" *Ave maris stella*"—" Hail star of the sea"—is sung in her honour, or to procure her favour. At the first verse all go on their knees, as is done at the verse, " *O crux ave*"—" Hail! O! cross," when chanting the hymn " *Vexilla Regis*" in honour of the cross—a posture of adoration unheeded when hymns are sung in honour of God.

What a multitude of odd ceremonies is connected with the use of holy water. It is astonishing what virtue is ascribed to this consecrated element. Nothing can be blessed or hallowed without it; neither candles, nor new fruits, nor new-laid eggs, nor ships, nor dwelling-houses, nor churches, nor bells, nor sacerdotal vestments. It is used in the administration of all the sacraments, before mass and after mass, and at the churching of women. Nothing, in short, can be done without holy water. Even the butter-churn is sprinkled with it before the churning commences, that the cream might work the better. It purifies the air, heals distempers, cleanses the soul, expels Satan and his imps from haunted houses, and introduces the Holy Ghost as an inmate in their stead. It is generally believed that the holy water blessed at Easter and Christmas, possesses superior virtue, on which account several tubs or barrels full must be blessed upon these occasions, in order to supply the increased demand. Protestants being quite incredulous as to the miraculous virtues ascribed to holy water, have abolished the use of it, and are of opinion that it bears a strong resemblance to the lustral water that was commonly used in the rites of pagan superstition.

Salt in like manner is pressed into the ceremonial of religion, probably because in the New Testament the apostles were called the salt of the earth. It is blessed for a variety of purposes. After being, first of all, duly exorcised itself, it is made use of in the administration of baptism and in the manufacture of holy water.

The ceremonial of blessing the oils—the *oleum infirmorum*, the oil for the sick, the *oleum cathecumenorum*, the oil for catechumens, and the *chrisma* or *chrism*, is complicated beyond measure, and magnificent withal. On Maunday Thursday it is consecrated by the bishop, robed in his pontificals, in the presence of the diocesan clergy, robed in their vestments; who all, at the appointed times, while it is in progress of consecration, worship it by triple genuflection, salutation, and psalmody!!! The holy oil is adored on Maunday Thursday, just as the cross is on Good Friday; on which latter occasion also, a multiplicity of odd ceremonies takes place.

The worship of inanimate things is justified on the score of its being merely relative; that is, referable to something really entitled to our adoration. There may be some reason in this. But what object of this kind is there to which the adoration of the oils may be referred?

The efficacy of this benediction lasts but for one

year ; at the expiration of which, it is understood that the holy oil becomes unfit to *communicate grace*, and should be committed for combustion to the devouring element of fire. The solemn consecration by the bishop, backed by a multitude of crosses and insufflations, &c. &c., performed by the body of priests in attendance, proves insufficient to protect it from the injuries of time and the decay of nature; just as happens to the consecrated host, which, when it happens to suffer decomposition, is acknowledged to be nothing more than decayed bread, unfit to nourish either body or soul.

Nothing can exceed the complication and multitude of the ceremonies observed in the conferring of holy orders ; which, though reckoned one individual sacrament and of a spiritual nature, is, like matter, divisible *ad infinitum*. You have particular ceremonies for the consecration of a pope, for the consecration of a patriarch, for the consecration of an archbishop, for the consecration of a bishop, for the consecration of an abbot, for the ordination of a priest, for the ordination of a deacon, for the ordination of a sub-deacon, for the collation of the four minor orders of reader, of porter, of acolite, of exorcist, and, finally, for giving the *prima tonsura*. What a tremendous ceremonial ! ! ! What a cumbrous machinery of religion ! ! and from such simple beginnings.

Religion, indeed, was overloaded with extravagancies at an early period. St. Augustine complains of the vast increase of whimsical ceremonies in his time. He says, "things in this respect had arrived at such a pitch of absurdity, that Christianity, which was freed from the servitude of the ceremonial law, had become more enslaved than Judaism itself—that, in short, the simplicity of the gospel had been forgotten." If this saint were alive at the present day, he would have infinitely more reason to complain on this score. Many Catholic theologians are of the same opinion with the holy father; but have not the same honesty or courage to give publicity to their sentiments. Thus it is that, between the connivance or timidity of some and the interested imposture of others, the errors of the ignorant are confirmed, and true religion lies buried beneath an accumulated weight of extravagance, absurdity, and superstition.

CHAPTER XXIV.

OF CONFESSION.

AURICULAR confession furnishes matter for disputation between the two churches. A special confession of sins is recommended in the Protestant liturgy.* Protestantism, however, does not consider it as a divine institution. This was the opinion of Erasmus, and of the schoolmen of the middle ages. The Council of Trent, nevertheless, defined, that it is a precept established by divine authority. This was going very far in a question which, up to that time, had been considered at best but problematical. A distinction even still is made on the subject. There is, it is said, an ecclesiastical precept, and a divine precept, enjoining auricular confession. The ecclesiastical precept was issued by the fourth Council of Lateran, under Innocent the Third, imposing an obligation of annual confession. When, and under what circumstances, the divine precept is obligatory is a question not well cleared up. Estius was of opinion, that whoever confesses once in his whole life satisfies this obligation. This is nearly equivalent to the admission, that there is no divine precept for the practice.

* Vide Visitation of the Sick.

It is admitted that there is no specification of this precept in the New Testament ; but that it is implied in the commission given to the church, of binding and loosing, of forgiving and retaining sins ; for that otherwise this power could not be duly exercised. An argument of implication or expediency is a bad foundation on which to build a dogma of faith. St. James admonishes Christians to confess to one another. This monition of the apostle does not sustain the divine institution of auricular confession. The confession here recommended is mutual. In this case, if there be an obligation on the part of the people to make confession to the priests, there is likewise an obligation on the part of the priests to make confession to the people, an observance that would not prove very palatable. Moreover, the apostle does not say whether the confession should be of a special or of a general kind ; whether the sins should be acknowledged in detail and circumstantially, or be included in one single comprehensive accusation ; whether the confession should be private or public ? In short, no good argument, either positive or negative, can be deduced from the New Testament to prove, that auricular confession, as it is prescribed by the Roman Catholic church, was instituted by Jesus Christ.

In the writings of the early fathers, very little is said on the subject. Origen, in his third homily, reckons it among the remedies for sin ; but speaks not a word of its pre-eminence or necessity. It was successively established and suppressed in the church of Constantinople. The suppression was occasioned by the scandalous profligacy of the public confessor or penitentiary, who was discovered to have debauched one of his fair penitents in the very church where he sat to hear confessions. There is reason to fear that this profligacy of the Constantinopolitan penitentiary has been often imitated since that time. The suppression here mentioned, took place under Nectarius, the immediate predecessor of St. John Chrysostom, whose homilies before and after that event, speak different language on the subject of confession. In the former, confession is recommended : in the latter he insists on the propriety of confessing to God alone. The practice, however, in process of time, became very general; the result of taste, or a particular turn of devotion, or of the recommendation of the clergy, to whom it brought a prodigious accession of influence and emolument.

However, it had no fixedness or permanency until the time of Pope Innocent the Third, in the thirteenth century, under whom, in the fourth Council of Lateran, annual confession was enjoined under severe penalties, namely, of excommunication and interdict, in virtue of which the unfortunate prevaricator, in this particular, was cut off from the church, and denied, after death, the rites of Christian sepulture. This canon or rule, which is said to be still in force, has, notwithstanding, become a dead letter, as to the penal portion of it. The church, owing to the many humiliations she has undergone since the thirteenth century, has relaxed very much in the severity of her discipline ; so much so, that though she sees multitudes of her disobedient children living in the criminal neglect of this great duty, she still does not bar them entrance into the temple, nor deny them the rites of Christian burial. Her weakness shudders before the mighty ones of the world, among which supercilious class are to be found abundance of these disobedient children.

This subject, which is connected with that of penance and justification, has given employment to many profound theologians. There are elaborate disquisitions on the matter and form which the sacrament of penance, in common with the other six, must of necessity possess ; upon attrition and contrition, the latter of which reconciles the sinner without confession ; and upon the conditions which the validity of these mental affections require, upon the share which the fear of hell, and fear servilely servile take in this important process ; upon the jurisdiction requisite to qualify or authorize a priest to hear confessions at all ; upon approbation and reservation ; upon conditional, deprecatory, and absolute absolution ; upon satisfaction, whether it be an essential or only an accidental part of the sacrament ; upon the obligation of going to confession, though there should be no sins to confess; whether friars be fully privileged by the Pope to hear confessions, or have further occasion to receive special license for that purpose from the bishop of the diocess where they are located? Whether a parish priest may hear the confessions of strangers without license from their own parish priest, &c. &c.? These questions, so many, so intricate, so obscure, so controverted, cast a gloomy shade of uncertainty on the efficacy of confession, and are sufficient to make reflecting Christians come to the conclusion that their salvation, if coupled with a rite, whose validity depends upon such a multiplicity of subtleties and extravagancies, to say nothing of individual caprice, must be involved in alarming uncertainty.

There are some good confessors, no doubt, learned, religious, discreet men, who endeavour to inspire their penitents with a hatred of vice and a love of virtue. If all confessors were of this description, confession would be a wholesome practice. But this is not the case. The confessional becomes the medium of numberless abuses in the hands of the ignorant, the inexperienced, and the profligate. The doctrine of wrong is often inculcated instead of the doctrine of right; the knowledge of vice is conveyed by indelicate interrogatories, and the profligate priest makes the confessional subservient to the gratification of his unruly appetites. The crime "*solicitatio mulieris in tribunali*"—" to solicit a female in the tribunal"—is not of such rare occurrence, and would be very common, but for the dread of detection.

The present priest of the Ovens, who occupies the author's place, refused to give absolution to one of his (the author's) female servants, unless she quitted his employment. What did this come to? To pass by the injury attempted against the author himself, it was the same thing as to tell the poor girl, that she contracted the guilt of mortal sin by dwelling under his (the author's) roof. This the gentleman himself (who is a good judge of such matters) knew could not be the case. But he availed himself of the pernicious privilege he enjoys as a confessor, and of the weakness and ignorance of the poor girl, to gratify his bigoted or malicious propensities. He also makes it a bar to confession or absolution, that is, a mortal sin, for a father to send his children to a certain excellent school in the neighbourhood, for no other reason but that the master is not a Roman Catholic, and under his own control. He makes it also a crime not to join in the anti-tithe combination, and a virtue to obstruct the regular course of law. But he does not stand alone; all his fraternity, a few excepted, act a similar part.

A priest in the chair of confession is the most arbitrary of judges. He acts without check or control. His admonitions, his commands, his decisions, his casuistry, are not the necessary result of fixed principles or acknowledged maxims; but of his own particular qualities or dispositions; of his caprice; of his ignorance; of his prejudices; of his perversity; of his profligacy. Yet confession, under all these forbidding circumstances, is announced, is trumpeted as a necessary means of salvation—*a secunda post naufragium tabula*, "a second plank after ship-wreck;" and the favour of heaven, the grace of God, the justification of the sinner, is restricted, as an adjunct, to human precariousness and profanation!

But how is this machinery of confession made to work? how is it brought into action? In the country the poor people practise confession, for the most part, through dread of public exposure. And how do they practise it? How do they prepare for it? When they hear of the priest's arrival at the station-house, they quit their labour in the field or in the barn, hurry to the confessor, make a compendious recital of some sins they are in the constant habit of committing, and confessing, make some sort of a promise of amendment, as a matter of routine, receive absolution, hear the mass recited in Latin, take the blessed sacrament, pay the confession dues or battle with the priest, return to their labour with an obligation of repeating a number of rosaries within a given time, and think no more of the transaction. In the cities and large towns, confession is very generally neglected, except at the point of death.

Does confession improve the morals? It is said that a bad confession or a confession not clothed with the necessary conditions, not accompanied by a change of disposition and a firm purpose of amendment, superinduces the guilt of sacrilege, and adds immeasurably to the guilt of the pretended penitent. Must not this take place in most instances, from the mode in which confession is practised; and if so, what improvement in public morals can result from it? But this is only a theoretical argument. Let the question be decided by general facts. Are those who practise confession better conducted or less immoral than those who do not? Are they better husbands, better fathers, better subjects, better citizens, less given to turbulence, to sedition, to lying, to injustice? Have the Roman Catholics the advantage of the Reformers in this respect? Compare nations together. Confession is universally practised in Spain and Portugal. It is not practised in England or Scotland. Is the state of morality, public and private, among the Spaniards and Portuguese higher in the scale of virtue than among Englishmen and Scotchmen? What was the state of morals throughout Christendom in the times of old when the benefits or evils of this practice were universally felt? History will not give a very creditable answer to the question. Will any one venture to say that the Irish Catholics, who go to confession at stations twice a year or once a year, as they would to a fair or pattern, are superior in virtue and good manners, to their Protestant fellow countrymen, who learn their Christian duties from the Sacred Scriptures? Or that the Spaniards, and Portuguese, and Italians, are superior as men and as Christians, to the people of England or Scotland, or Holland, or the Protestant states of Germany? Or that the Roman Catholics, taken collectively and individually, do not lose considerably by the comparison? And if so, is it right that malevolent, profligate priests,—and many there are of this revolting description—should be enabled with impunity to lay snares for innocence, and to break into the sanctuary of private life, and make it a matter of conscience with weak-minded servants and labourers to ruin the interests of a good master and employer? If confession is at all to be practised, let not faculties be given indiscriminately to all, but only to such as are of approved experience, approved knowledge, and approved integrity. But where are such persons to be found? and to whom are we giving advice? "*Canitur surdo.*" We are piping to the deaf.

CHAPTER XXV.

ON FASTING AND ABSTINENCE.

In regard to fasting and abstinence the two churches are fast gravitating towards one another. The Catholic church is becoming Protestant in this respect. Christian perfection was at one time thought to consist in austerity. It was said by a witty physician in Germany, who lived shortly after the time of the first Reformers, that, but for an honest man, one Martin Luther, who had providentially appeared among them, they would have been feeding before that time on dry hay, like the cattle. The tide of orthodoxy is now fast setting against all severity in church discipline. Fast days are fast disappearing from the calendar, and the probability is, that even the discipline of celibacy will, at no distant period, be modified, or perhaps abolished altogether. Among the Roman Catholics in South America, there is no law of abstinence. In the Catholic countries on the continent of Europe, it is nearly the same case ; and in Ireland, rapid strides have been made, within these few years, to the same state of Christian liberty. It is to be hoped we shall soon see an end of fantastical, contradictory, episcopal regulations in this particular ; for example : permitting the use of fleshmeat in the diocess of Cloyne, and prohibiting it in the diocess of Cork ; so that an innocent act on the beach of Cove, would be criminal if performed on Rocky Island. The better order of Catholics this long time past have lived, in this respect, like their Protestant neighbours ; and the Catholic priests themselves, the expounders of the law, generally left to others the fulfilment of it. Let us say a few words on the general question.

Abstinence, as a precept, is, according to Scripture, coeval with man. Adam and Eve were interdicted the fruit of a certain tree, called the tree of knowledge, of good and evil; and the violation of this interdict so displeased the Almighty that he expelled the disobedient pair from the garden of paradise, and made them obnoxious to all the misfortunes now incidental to human nature. A precept was delivered to Noah immediately after the deluge, interdicting mankind the use of flesh with blood. The old law included numberless abstinential precepts; some regarding the community at large; others regarding particular classes, which, however, as being nothing more than positive injunctions, affected only the Jewish people, and were all finally abrogated by the coming of Jesus Christ, the founder of the new law.

The abolition of these ancient ordinances was not followed by the institution of new ones of a similar kind. The body of doctrine preached by the Messiah included no precept of abstinence. It is true that the apostles, assembled in council at Jerusalem, drew up a monitory instruction, in which they besought the converted Gentiles of Antioch to abstain from things strangled and from blood. But this was a mere temporary regulation adopted for the purpose of satisfying the prejudices of the converted Jews, who, in embracing the gospel, still foolishly imagined themselves not freed from the injunctions of the Levitical law. The precepts of abstinence, which are now imposed, are consequently of mere ecclesiastical authority. Some, no doubt, are of such antiquity, that we cannot well ascertain the date of their origin. It is highly probable that customs of this kind have always pervaded, and that the progress of time did nothing more than to alter the mode of observance. St. Paul says, that to avoid scandalizing a weak brother, he avoided partaking of certain meats; so that through fear of giving offence to the weak minded, he abstained from that which in itself and under other circumstances was perfectly harmless. These weak persons were Jewish proselytes; and it may be said that the custom first, and afterwards the precept, of abstaining was in some sort a continuation of the old abstinential precepts contained in the Jewish ceremonial law. But it may be asked, was the Christain church warranted in copying after the Jewish institute, in the enacting of laws similar to those that had been abrogated by her divine Founder? Did not the repeal or annulment take place by divine authority? And was church authority sufficient for their re-enactment? The Jews are ridiculed because they abstain from swine's flesh through a motive of religion. Is it not more ridiculous for Christians to abstain, on certain days and during certain seasons, not only from swine's flesh but from every kind and description of fleshmeat? Temperance is the great cardinal virtue commanded in the gospel, which interdicts, without distinction, all manner of gluttony and excess.

Jesus Chirst, as we may learn from St. Matthew, fasted forty days and forty nights, in commemoration of which fast or abstinence the forty days fast of Lent, it is said, was instituted. This prodigious fast of our Saviour should be numbered among his miracles, as human nature of itself could never undergo so lasting a privation. Now, it may be fairly asked, are we under any obligation to imitate him in the performance of miracles? His example in respect to all such matters was not intended for imitation but to produce conviction. He did not forget to particularize on what he was to be considered as our model and example. "Learn of me, (said he,) to be meek and humble of heart." Abstinence or temperance is a check upon the unruly appetites, and, as such, is recommended in many passages of the New Testament.

The Pythagorians of old never eat flesh. The Indian Brahmins observe the same abstinence at the present day. The Roman Catholics at times transform themselves into Pythagorians or Brahmins. How all the world occasionally harmonizes! The Protestant calendar marks down, for fasting and abstinence, the forty days of Lent, a number of vigils, ember days, rogation days, and every Friday in the year. As to the letter it is the same with the Roman calendar. The Protestants of the olden time were, many of them, strict enough in this particular; but those of the present day have shaken off the austerity of their predecessors, and reduced to a dead letter all their abstinental rubricks. Relaxation, in short, in this respect, is the general order of the day; and it seems to be at length agreed on all hands, that true religion does not necessarily imply distinction of meats or subtraction of nutriment, but holiness of life.

Who'd think endued with common sense,
That bacon slice gives God offence;
Or that a herring has the charm
Almighty vengeance to disarm;
Wrapt up in majesty divine,
Does he regard on what we dine?—SWIFT.

CHAPTER XXVI.

ON PURGATORY.

THE doctrine of purgatory makes no inconsiderable noise in the arena of religious controversy. Many strange opinions are held relative to the geography of the invisible world. Besides hell, heaven, and purgatory, we have a spiritual prison or enclosure for unbaptised infants, and the *limbus patrum*, to which some add "the bosom of Abraham," into which Lazarus was carried, a sort of second-rate heaven. Of all these extra places, purgatory is the most celebrated. Considerable difference of opinion exists upon this subject. The Latins or Roman Catholics have one kind of purgatory, the

Greeks another, and the reformers no purgatory at all. The first believe that purgatory is a sort of hell, where the souls of the faithful departed are tortured by fire; the second deny this, but say it is a place of darkness and privation; the last, by laying the axe to the root of the controversy, are freed from the disagreeable necessity of entering into any such horrifying particulars.

The belief of the easterns seems to be the offspring of a doctrine of very ancient standing—that the souls of the faithful were not to enter heaven, or into the realms of light, until after the general judgment. This opinion, like millenarianism, was entertained very generally in the early ages of Christianity, and is not without many abettors at the present day.

The Roman church admits, that no one is bound to believe that purgatory, like hell, is a place of fire and flame, or that the Greeks are to be condemned for saying that it is a place of darkness. This doctrine of the Greeks corresponds, indeed, to the *memento* for the dead made in the canon of the Latin mass, where prayer is made, "that God may introduce such as rest in Christ into a place of refreshment, *light*, and peace." However, the doctrine constantly preached by the priests and friars is, that the poor souls in purgatory are enveloped in flame, and suffer, like Dives, the most excruciating torture; and that to relieve them from this calamity, masses, for which money is paid, are most efficacious. This is not only to make the doctrine of purgatory an article of faith, but also an article of merchandize; and, contrary to the admonition of St. Paul, to teach that which is unseemly, for the sake of filthy lucre.

Some attempt to prove purgatory from the words of our Saviour in St. Matthew; when speaking of the sin against the Holy Ghost, he says, "it will not be forgiven either in this world or in the world to come." If they fancy that this text has any reference to purgatory, they must admit that it is a place of expiation for mortal sins. What is read in the book of Maccabees concerning sacrifices for the dead possesses little authority in the matter for two reasons—that the book itself is not accounted canonical, and consequently, as Gregory the Great said, cannot be quoted to prove a matter of faith; and secondly, because what it says on the subject receives no confirmation or countenance from any passage in Leviticus, which observes a profound silence on this torturing subject.

The holy fathers say not a word about the fire of purgatory. The fact is, they denied the existence of any such place. St. John Chrysostom, in his fourteenth homily on St. Matthew, affirms that after death no mercy, but rigid justice is to be expected. "There is no *middle place* (said he) between hell and heaven." This language cannot be misunderstood. Even in the beginning of the sixth century, the doctrine of purgatory was little known. St.

Fulgentius, in answer to a question proposed by Euthemius, namely, whether God remits sins in this life only ?—declared in the affirmative. "After this life, (he says,) there is no intermediate state between punishment and reward ; that rigid justice only will be exercised in the world to come." He either rejected the doctrine of purgatory, or he knew nothing of it, for he speaks without qualification or exception.

The prayers, which it was customary even in the early ages to offer for the dead, did not suppose a second state of suffering for souls departed, but were the result of excessive regard for deceased friends or relatives; and of a hope or expectation that such prayers may possibly contribute to procure for them a more favourable judgment, whenever the time of trial should arrive; concerning which period or moment, the ideas of the early Christians were exceedingly confused.

Under all these circumstances, with so much uncertainty hanging about it, the east and west are at variance on the subject ; the Roman church admitting a latitude of opinion respecting it, and at the same time not admitting such latitude by preaching the doctrine of purging fire; not resting on any foundation of Scripture or ancient tradition, on the contrary discountenanced by both; under such circumstances, should the doctrine of purgatory be made an essential or integral part of orthodoxy ; or should those Christians be branded with the mark of heresy who reject it altogether? But then, if assent be given to the reformers on this point, what will become of mortuary masses and all the emoluments thence arising? This is a difficulty in the subject not to be got over.

CHAPTER XXVII.

ON THE INVOCATION OF SAINTS.

Dr. Milner, in his "End of Controversy," admits that the practice of praying to the saints is not of imperative obligation; and that, strictly speaking, we are bound only to pray to God. This important admission, which only echoes the opinion of George Cassander and other Catholic doctors, cannot be reconciled with the practice of the Roman church; for, praying to the saints, though thus accounted a matter of indifference, is completely incorporated with the Roman Catholic religion. The saints and angels are addressed upon all, even the most solemn occasions; are indeed constantly associated in worship with the Deity. If the Pope issues a bull or encyclical letter, he always concludes by invoking the blessed Virgin, Mother of God, and the blessed Apostles, Peter and Paul, the titular saints of the Vatican. At confession, the penitent sets out by acknowledging his guiltiness, not only to God, but also to the Virgin, and a number of the most distinguished saints, whom he names individually; and the saints also share with the Deity the homage offered in the sacrifice of the mass.

Extra-privileges are annexed to the various festivals instituted in honour of the Virgin, and to the festivals of the other saints, on which occasions a larger measure of grace is attainable than on other occasions, when the worship of the Deity is more free from intermixture. Besides the blessed Virgin, who is supposed to possess a pre-eminence of celestial influence, many other individual saints are looked up to with great confidence by many pious votaries, and are considered as undoubted securities to them for their future salvation. Among these we may make special mention of St. Augustine, St Francis of Assisium, and St. Dominic Gusman. The friars of the several orders, that take their designation from these celebrated saints, are constantly trumpeting, in the ears of the devout, the religious benefits that result from an adherence to their respective rituals, and from the payment of due honours to their beatified patrons. Indulgences innumerable, and of peculiar efficacy, are promised to the pious votary; and the followers of these newfangled rites are under the impression, that they can attain heaven much more easily and securely than if they had confined themselves to the original institutes of Christianity. In short, what with indulgences, and habits, and cords, and scapulars, and rosaries, and processions, and litanies to the Virgin and to the saints, and the multitude of prayers addressed to them on such occasions, religious worship is diverted from the great God, and religious hope or expectation is made to centre in the creature rather than in the Creator. Thus it is, that what is acknowledged to be a matter of indifference by Dr. Milner and others, is, by a rare combination of weakness and craft, converted, in the eye of ignorance, into the essence of religion, and the theory of Catholic theologians is at variance with the usages of the Catholic church. Is there not a loud demand in this particular for the pruning knife of retrenchment and reform ?

Image worship stands much upon a footing with the practice of praying to the saints. It is carried to great lengths, and leads to great abuses in the Roman Catholic countries on the continent. In short, between the mediatorship of saints and the worship of images, Roman Catholic Christianity is likened to Paganism. Image worship is less defensible than praying to saints ; for it was expressly condemned in the old law, and the damnatory precept is retained under the new covenant. It was not till after the lapse of some centuries that it began to be introduced among Christians. It spread gradually, became general, and gave, for a time, considerable scandal ; so much so, that under Leo the Isaurian, in the eastern church, it was condemned and abolished by the authority of a council held at Constantinople, consisting of three hundred bishops. This state of things, however, did not continue long. Image worship had still its abettors ; a reaction took place in its favour, and under the Empress Irene, the cotemporary of Charlemagne, a council, which assembled at Nice, after much labour and debate, annulled the decision of Constantinople, and restored image worship.

The acts of this council, however, did not meet the approbation of the western church. The emperor Charles the Great, who was fond of intermeddling in ecclesiastical affairs, assembled a numerous council at Frankfort, where it was decided that the acts of this Nicene Synod were "destitute of *common sense!*" All this took place so late as the close of the eighth century ; a proof that a very serious and protracted opposition was made to the introduction and establishment of image worship. Are the Reformers wrong, therefore, in rejecting it ? or are Roman Catholics justified in blending it with orthodoxy ? The premises laid down will furnish the answer. We shall conclude with a quotation from Bossuet,* who, writing on this subject, has the following words :—"It is true,

* Vide his Expositions on the Catholic Faith, 4th chapter.

that, as the exterior marks of reverence are not absolutely necessary, the church could, without altering her doctrine, extend or confine these practices as the exigencies of times would seem to require, not wishing that her children should be tied down servilely to visible objects."

CHAPTER XXVIII.

OF THE SCAPULAR.

THE anonymous author of a miserable publication, which lately made its appearance in Cork, and is miscalled "A Reply to our Essay on Finance," seems greatly offended at the liberty we have taken to denounce as consecrated trumpery, scapulars, habits, cords and *Agnus Deis*. This pitiable scribbler, who, it appears, acted only as amanuensis to the Roman Catholic bishop, Dr. Murphy, has contributed to give publicity to a gallimafry of bad grammar, bad logic, bad theology, heresy,* malice, bigotry, falsehood, and misrepresentation. This clandestine scribbler has become the dupe of the priests, and is made at their instance the foul vehicle of filth and nonsense and calumny.

From the exceptions that have been taken against us by this learned mouthpiece of orthodox episcopacy, and the corresponding outcry of priests and friars, and the joint yells of the various packs of holy confraternities, it should be taken for granted, that we have attempted to mislead the public in these particulars; and that scapulars, habits, &c. &c., notwithstanding what we have said to the contrary, do constitute an essential portion of the Irish Roman Catholic religion. Let us examine this matter a little.

Before the times of Simon Stock, of Francis of Assisium, of Dominic Gusman, and of Nicholas Tolentinus, all these important appendages of religion were unknown. In the thirteenth century, which many good and wise men account an age of darkness, the three former of these remarkable

* He says that a schismatical church cannot communicate grace. In this case baptism by heretics is invalid. This is contrary to the doctrine of the church of Rome.

personages made their appearance, and shed new light on the gospel dispensation ; so that the church had subsisted for upwards of twelve centuries in a state of comparative darkness and imperfection. Scapulars were then introduced by Simon Stock, cords by St. Francis, habits by St. Dominic; and after a lapse of some time, little blessed loaves, by Nicholas Tolentine. The Carmelites, of which holy brotherhood Simon Stock was a distinguished member, gave currency to the scapular, the Dominicans of course to the holy habit, the Franciscans to the cord, and the Augustinians to the bread of St. Nicholas. Thus each particular order had a peculiar spiritual good to diffuse among the body of the faithful—a happy arrangement, for it operated at once as a preventive to confusion, and a bar to the evil consequences of religious monopoly. The regular clergy, or friars, as they are called, have been always laudably attentive to their duty in these important matters. They zealously inculcate the utility or necessity of this new species of devotion, these new and powerful helps to salvation. Nevertheless, the success of their labours has not come up to the full measure of their hopes and expectations. The enlightened and well-informed have continued to pursue the old beaten track of religious devotion; indeed all persons of religion and discernment do the same; so that the votaries of this novel species of Christianity are to be found principally among the lowest, the weakest, and the most ignorant of the community ; are made up, most part of doating old women, of the wives and daughters of humble tradesmen, labourers and small farmers, together with a slight sprinkling of the male population, who may be affected by the hypocondriacs. With all these the blessed scapular, which is called the garment of the Virgin, is held in mighty veneration. This takes the lead and leaves at an immeasurable distance in the rear, the habit of Dominic, and the cord of Francis—a circumstance that brings superabundance of grist to the mill of the Carmelites, to whom appertains of right the benediction and distribution of this sacred livery.

The spiritual advantages annexed to the scapular are said to be immense. It carries in its train graces in abundance ; is indeed a complete foil to all the insidious attacks of the arch-enemy of mankind. The scapularians themselves are fully persuaded that it will save them from the gulf of perdition, and open to them a safe and speedy passage to the realms above. Under these circumstances the scapular challenges our peculiar attention, and deserves to be particularly considered. We shall therefore take a cursory review of a treatise that has been written on the subject, and not long since reprinted, like Peter Dens, in Dublin, "*cum permissu superiorum*," for the instruction and edification of the Irish faithful.

The scapular is a square or oblong bit of stuff resembling a flat pincushion, marked thus with the initials I.H.S. It is suspended by a ribbon or a string from the neck, after the manner of an eye or quizzing glass, but worn inside. It must be made, as the author of the scapular book says, of cloth, serge, or other stuff, and not of silk. It may, however, he says, be lined with silk, and embroidered with gold and silver. This is a combination of opposites, of plainness with gaudiness, of beggary with grandeur, and humility with pride. A very substantial reason is assigned for the homeliness of the chief material, namely, that the blessed Virgin never wore silk, but always woollen, and that too of its original colour,—that is, as it came from the sheep's back. This example, our author says, should be imitated by the votaries of the scapular, who are called her devout children. This is all very well, as to the woollen stuff used for the body of the scapular, or the substratum, but how can the silk lining, and the gold and silver embroidery, be reconciled to the plain and coarse habiliments of the virgin mother? So much for the matter, and form, and decorations of the scapular. Let us now inquire into its history.

Simon Stock was the favoured individual through whom this heavenly gift was transmitted to mankind.

England, it appears, has the honour of having given birth to this celebrated personage. He was born in the county of Kent, in the year 1165. Arrived at the age of twelve, which is a mystical number, he withdrew into a neighbouring forest, where he lived for twenty years in the practice of great austerity, and in the perpetual exercise of celestial meditations. He had for his dwelling or his lodging, the hollow trunk of an old oak—which circumstance procured him the odd surname of Stock—and for his food wild roots and herbs. On festival days, however, he fared somewhat better; for on these occasions an inspired spaniel, or pointer, or terrier, or an inspired dog of some description, brought safely in his mouth, to our hungry hermit, bread sufficient for a present repast. This circumstance is somewhat marvellous. A dog is employed as a special messenger of heaven, to carry holiday fare to Simon Stock, waiting its arrival in the hollow trunk of an aged oak. The great Saint John the Baptist was not favoured in this extraordinary manner. Let us go on. In this retreat, says the writer, Simon received many supernatural graces from the Almighty, and enjoyed the familiar conversation of the blessed Virgin. The story of the carrier dog has nothing of the marvellous, if compared to this. The blessed Virgin holding familiar converse with Simon Stock in his wooden bower; quitting the heavenly Jerusalem to beguile the hours of a young hermit; dividing her time between him and the celestials!!! Happy Simon, seated in his oaken cavity, infinitely more happy than Diogenes in his tub. The philosopher had once the honour of a visit from Alexander of Macedon; but what was Alexander of Macedon, compared to the Queen of Heaven, who deigned to become the constant visitor of the redoubted Simon?

After such supernatural agency as this, what becomes of the celebrated precept of Horace, in his art of poetry,

> Nec Deus intersit nisi dignus vindice nodus
> Inciderit.

> Never presume to make a God appear,
> But for a business worthy of a God.—ROSCOMMON.

But let us not stray from Simon, who was not to be tied down to the ordinary rules of rational beings. We find that he was furnished with things terrestrial through the ministry of a dog, and with things celestial through the agency of the Virgin Mary. All these favours were, however, mere preliminaries to the inestimable donation of the scapular, through the instrumentality of which such a profusion of graces was to be poured upon a sinful world. This great boon was received from the very hands of the Virgin by holy Simon, on the 16th of July, 1251, in the Carmelite Convent of Cambridge, in the following surprising manner:—"As he was upon his knees in the oratory (all alone it appears) the most glorious Virgin, environed with celestial splendour, attended by thousands of angels, appeared before him; and, holding the sacred scapular in her hand, addressed him thus—'Receive, most beloved son, the scapular of thy order, a sign of my confraternity, a privilege both to thee and to all Carmelites, in which whoever dieth shall not suffer *eternal fire*. Behold the sign of salvation, a safeguard in danger, the covenant of peace and everlasting alliance.' " There is nothing in the records of religion surpassing the magnificence of this spectacle. The heavens open, the virgin mother descends environed with splendour, and with myriads of angels in her train—like the coming of Christ in the clouds at the last day to judge the world;—she enters the oratory where Simon was at prayer, hands him the scapular—that is, a square bit of woollen stuff, cut out and stitched, of course, either by herself or by ministering angels—and declares this same bit of woollen stuff to be the sure and certain pledge of all manner of heavenly graces, favours, and immunities. The appearance of the angels to the shepherds on the night of the nativity of our Lord, his transfiguration on Mount Tabor, his resurrection from the dead, his ascension into heaven, the descent of the Holy Ghost, the most splendid scene, in short, recorded in the New Testament, does not equal the supernatural grandeur that accompanied the delivery of a little woollen rag into the hands of the Carmelite Simon.

What say ye to all this, ye preachers of the gospel, seculars and regulars?—ye oracles of infallibility; ye who denominate your pulpits the chairs of truth, and sometimes denounce lying and falsehood as the offspring of Satan? Are ye not convinced of the falsehood of what is here related concerning Simon Stock and this scapular?—that it is all the work or the invention of some sacrilegious impostor or impostors, to delude, to cajole, and to cozen? And if, under this persuasion, instead of disabusing the weak-minded upon a matter of such serious moment, you labour to perpetuate the sacrilegious delusion, what are ye but the ministers of deceit, and the apostles of falsehood? Do ye act as ministers of God, or as the ministers of Satan, when, contrary to your own persuasion, you teach the people, or suffer the people to rest their hopes of salvation upon what may well be designated the very consummation of religious jugglery and imposture?

But let us pursue the story of the scapular. Losing sight for the moment of old Simon, let us bring Pope John the 22d on the stage, as an actor in this sacrilegious drama. The blessed Virgin appeared to this man, while yet a cardinal, and promised him the chair of St. Peter, provided he pledged himself that, when elevated to the papal dignity, to favour her children of the scapular, and to confirm on earth "what her beloved son, at *her particular request*, had ratified in heaven," namely, "that all who wear her habit—the scapular—should be absolved from the *third part* of their sins, (why not from the entire?) and if after death they should chance to go to purgatory, that she—the most holy Virgin—would deliver them thence on the first Saturday after their decease." What in all the "*materia religiosa*" can be compared to the scapular after all this? It ensures the remission of sins, and a speedy enlargement from the prison of purgatory. What virtue in a two-inch square bit of serge, or frize, or cassimere, or ratteen, or broad cloth! Talk no more of Pacolet's horse, or of Poucet's seven-league boots, or the wishing-cap of Fortunatus, or the power of the steam engine.

Give me the holy scapular; the scapular for me. Let us go on. We find a more particular detail of its extraordinary virtues in the learned preface of this invaluable work. First, he says, "It is not of human institution, but *jure divino*, as theologians say." This appears from the celestial mode of its delivery, as we have seen—although a cavilling logician might say that, as the blessed Virgin from whom it is derived was only a human being, it cannot be proved to be of any other than of human institution;—but perhaps the Carmelites, like the Collyridians of old, accord her the privileges of a deity. The writer of the scapular book, indeed, asserts that she exercises command over Jesus Christ, and shares with him his omnipotence. But to the virtues of the scapular. "It has," he says, "the promise of eternal salvation annexed to it; it avails much to abbreviate the pains of purgatory." This falls somewhat short of the efficacy already ascribed to it in that respect. But these little slips are of small moment. Let us go on. "Ever since its first institution, it hath been always favoured by

Almighty God with many graces and miracles; insomuch that, by reason of the sacred scapular, the sick have been cured, persons bewitched and possessed (by the devil) have been freed, women in travail have been miraculously assisted. It also hath extinguished fires, when cast into the flame for that purpose. It hath appeased violent tempests, when cast into the sea in the time of danger. In fine, it is known by daily experience, that it is a sovereign remedy for all the evils of this life, both spiritual and temporal; insomuch, that the devils have been often heard to howl, saying—woe to us by reason of the sacred scapular of the blessed Virgin Mary of Mount Carmel." Bravo! the scapular. It beats Jack's skin of parchment; it is the philosopher's stone; it is the universal medicine. It extinguishes fires, visible and invisible; it checks inundations, stills the tempest, calms the raging sea, expels devils, and sets all hell in an uproar. It possesses the power of obstetrication; hastens parturition; cures the gout, the ague, the palsy, and the epilepsy; heals scalds, burns, bruises, and fractures, simple and compound; proves an effectual counteraction to spells, charms, and incantations. In a word, it is a sovereign specific for all the evils, spiritual and corporal, of mankind. What an invaluable boon is not this scapular! What a pity that due advantage is not taken of it!—that it is not employed for the benefit of individuals, and of society at large. What a great saving might be made through its instrumentality in the matter of insurance against dangers from fire, and dangers from the sea! This species of trafficking or dealing might in that case be done away with altogether. The scapular should remove every apprehension for life or property, arising from the devouring elements—from fires, inundations, and tempests; and all the interests of the state, commercial, agricultural, and manufacturing, be thus made to rest on a secure and satisfactory basis. Verily, Simon Stock, the whole world should do thee homage. And yet, so far from this being the case, that notwithstanding the providential care taken of thee by the carrier dog, thy familiar intercourse with the Virgin, thy miraculous reception of the scapular, and its happy and beneficial diffusion, by means of thee, through an ungrateful world, thy name is not, after all, to be found in the Roman Calendar. What is the cause of this omission? Was he considered as a saint, or was he regarded as an impostor? The Carmelites would exclaim blasphemy against the latter assertion. But let him be a saint, and let us come to some edifying particulars respecting the miraculous virtues of his scapular.

On the sixteenth of July, the very day on which the Virgin delivered it to Simon, he had occasion to go to Winchester, to transact some business with the bishop of that see. He had no sooner arrived there than the Dean of St. Helen's church waited on him, and besought him to pay a visit to his (the

Dean's) brother, Walter, who was dying in a state of desperation; insomuch that he would not hear the name of God mentioned, but continually invoked Satan to avenge him of some person who had mortally wounded him. The holy Simon immediately paid a visit to the unhappy Walter, whom he found deprived of all use of reason, grinding his teeth and rolling his eyes in a most terrific manner. Having first of all recommended him to God, as the story goes, Simon laid the scapular on the dying man, when, lo and behold you, the maniac, all at once, came to himself; every thing was set to rights *instanter*. He now abhorred the Devil, with whom he had before made a compact, begged pardon for his sins, made his confession, received all the rites of the church, and died that same night in all the odour of sanctity. But the Dean of St. Helen's being still in some doubt of poor Walter's salvation, having some misgivings on the subject, the dead man appeared to him and assured him that, owing to the virtues of the scapular, he had eluded all the snares of the Devil, and escaped everlasting damnation. Let us talk no more of the scapular, "*a priori*," or in the abstract. Here we view it brought into miraculous operation. Simon Stock, on the very day he received it, while yet new and fresh from the hands of the Virgin, seized an opportunity, that luckily offered, of trying its efficacy. He goes to the Bishop of Winchester, perhaps to narrate its wonderful delivery, to disclose the splendid interview he had been favoured with, and to exhibit to the admiring prelate the celestial scapular, the new help to salvation, the mystical badge, that had lain concealed from the beginning of the world, the great glory and ornament of the Carmelite order. Perhaps Simon exclaimed at the time with Horace, holding it up in his hand, "*O et presidium et dulce decus meum*"—"My safeguard and my glory." Well, Simon is unexpectedly called off from his business, or his interview with the bishop, to visit an unhappy man, who was dying in all the agonies of despair, grinding his teeth, rolling his eyes, cursing his enemies, and invoking the Devil, and who happened at the same time to be the brother of a dignitary of the church—no less a personage than the Dean of St. Helen's; and it was at the particular request also of this same dean, that our holy Carmelite visited the dying sinner. No doubt the clergy of Winchester, the dean and chapter, had all tried their skill upon poor Walter, had exorcised him, had offered prayers and sacrifices for him, and preached to him, and admonished him ; had employed all the armoury of religion to restore him to a sane mind ; but all their labours proved fruitless—the devil was too powerful, and still kept a fast grip of him. As a last resource, and when the despair of the dying maniac was in a manner communicated to the whole imbecile clerical body of Winchester : when, in fact, they had given the poor unfortunate culprit up as a bad job, and considered his damnation certain, Simon, the carmelite, is called in, bearing about him the holy scapular. The crisis was awful ; the efficacy of the scapular was put to the test ; but it came off victorious. Simon having just laid it on the demoniac, he was all at once cured of his impious frenzy. He no longer gnashed his teeth, nor rolled his eyes, nor cursed his enemies, nor invoked the Devil. The scapular altered instantaneously his whole frame of mind and body, and placed him in such a happy mood of devotion, that he expired that same night, cleansed, purified, and regenerated. It would appear, however, after all, that the melancholy dean still entertained some doubts respecting his deceased brother ; that he had fears for his salvation ; that he distrusted the full and absolute efficacy of the scapular ; that in opposition to the clearest testimony, he was still sceptical on the subject. Such a person would not believe Moses and the prophets. But his doubts were removed by the testimony of one who rose from the dead for that important purpose, which posthumous personage, to leave no further room for cavilling or ambiguity on the subject, was no other than the deceased Walter himself. As to the exact period of his re-appearance, authors are silent. We suppose little time was lost, as the question to be cleared up was of the last importance. Walter came from among the dead, and showed himself to the doubting dean, like as Samuel, roused by the witch of Endor, appeared to anxious Saul, assuring him that all was right ; for that the holy scapular had freed him from the gripe of Satan, and from eternal perdition. After this, who but a fool would run the risk of dying without a scapular ; and what a profanation it was in the author of the condemned pamphlet to characterize it as consecrated trumpery! It is no wonder that he has been made to feel all the effects of episcopal vengeance ; and to suffer, in rapid succession, the alarming penalties of denouncement, suspension, and deprivation. But to make our case still worse, we shall relate another scapularian miracle.

In the city of Avignon, in the year of our Lord 1622, that is to say, after a lapse of nearly 400 years from the days of Simon Stock, a person of rank, named Alexander Dominic, a native of Lyons, and an officer in the army, being on his way to join his regiment in the field, halted for some days to assist, with many others, in celebrating the great feast of the scapular. It happened that on the 10th of July, that is, six days before the festival in question, as he was just coming out from the bath, he was assaulted by a murderous adversary, who, cocking a loaded pistol at his breast, instantly discharged it, and lodged a pair of bullets in the unfortunate man's body. The poor cavalier, fancying himself mortally wounded, and that he had not a moment to live, had instant recourse to the great patroness of the confraternity, crying out "O! blessed Virgin of Mount Carmel assist me!" words which operated like magic; for he had no sooner uttered them, than, strange to say, he found that the pair of bullets had fallen down at once into his inexpressibles. He was forthwith removed to his lodgings, where, upon overhauling him, it was found that his cloak had been singed; that the bullets had passed through his doublet and shirt, and just grazed the holy scapular, which very fortunately he then wore next his skin. This miracle is not altogether so momentous as the first, when the scapular overmatched Satan and worked the salvation of a sinner. Here it secured the salvation of the body, by neutralizing the effects of gunpowder and fire-arms, and counteracting the combined forces of projection and gravitation. What a fortunate chevalier! He became pistol-proof by means of the scapular; which, far surpassing the armour of Achilles, rendered him all over invulnerable. What a happy halt he made on his way to the field of battle! How fortunate that he preferred the celebration of the Carmelite festival to the performance of his military duties!! This sacrifice of things earthly to things celestial procured for him the shield of celestial protection. How fortunate also, that in coming out of the bath he had not, in dressing himself, forgotten to suspend next his skin or next his heart, the holy scapular! For this was the mystical shield, against which the pistol bullets striking, were diverted from their murderous course, and, being turned into a new and safe direction, passed harmlessly down to the inexpressibles, to the inexpressible joy of poor terrified Alexander Dominic; for terrified he was beyond measure on this occasion, though a cavalier, as may appear from this circumstance, that, though he had not received the slightest wound, though he had been shot free, he still lost his locomotive powers, and was obliged to be borne, perhaps on a door, to his lodgings. There he was duly overhauled; his scapular was examined, as well as his shirt; his doublet, and his inexpressibles; and all present beheld, with mixed sensations of pleasure and astonishment, the miraculous peregrination or aberration of the two little harmless projectiles.

We shall trouble our readers with one miracle more out of a multitude wrought through means of the scapular. This took place at Toulon—a city in the south of France—in the year 1638, that is, about sixteen years after the miracle of the terrified cavalier. "A fire (as the author of the scapular book says) happened to break out in a street near the dwelling-house of a Mr. John Richard, advocate of parliament—(this is very circumstantial)—threatening speedy destruction to the whole neighbourhood. The lady of Mr. Richard, seeing that neither the efforts of the assembled multitude, nor the abundance of water poured on the devouring element could subdue its fury, bethought herself of casting into the flames the garment of the Virgin—the scapular—which was no sooner done than the fire not only abated of its fury but became all at once extinct." Here is a proof that the scapular possesses supreme command over the elements of fire and water; for it extinguished the former when the latter had been employed in vain for that purpose. But the author is silent as to what befel the scapular itself in this remarkable rencontre. In effecting the extinguishment of the flames, did it sustain itself any injury? Did it escape unhurt and undamaged? Or did it fall a sacrifice in the burning conflict, and die like Wolfe and Nelson in the arms of victory? But it would be an injury to the reputation of the scapular to suppose any thing like this. For if mutual destruction took place in the conflict, as nearly happened in the fight between the two cats, which devoured one another all but their tails, the question of victory would be a debateable point; and profane persons might be tempted to ask, how it happened that, while the scapular effected the preservation of pots, and kettles, and feather beds, it could not save itself from the devouring element. Perhaps it was lost through the ungrateful negligence of Mrs. Richard herself, who, when she saw all her goods and chattels in safety, thought no more on that which was the instrument of their preservation.

Neither should such carelessness be altogether condemned, for she was well aware how easily the lost scapular might be replaced :—

> Primo amisso non deficit alter.
>
> For well she wot the convent nigh,
> Would furnish her a new supply.

But to come more closely to the point, what, after all that we have seen, can be compared to the scapular? Can the mantle of Elias, which divided the waters of the Jordan; or the shadow of St. Peter, which cured the sick; or the kerchiefs and napkins of St. Paul, which put evil spirits to flight? By no means; for, as our author says, the scapular is the mantle or livery of the Blessed Virgin, before whom prophets and apostles fade away into utter insignificance.

Shall we still go on? Is it necessary to enter into all the minutiæ of this disgusting subject, or to dwell in lengthened detail on the mass of religious absurdities palmed by the high priests of the scapular—the order of Carmelites—on their silly credulous votaries? What can be more intolerable than the doctrines they teach concerning the Virgin Mary? They make her the great directrix over created nature, regulating, *ad libitum*, at pleasure, the fate of unhappy mortals in the visible and invisible world. They utterly degrade the Majesty of God—making him either a subordinate agent in the government of the world, or appear as if he regarded with indifference the usurpation of his authority. Let us quote a few precious passages to this effect from the scapular book. "There is no doubt, (it says,) but the Blessed Virgin Mary, by maternal right, is with Christ president of heaven and earth. It is fitting and convenient that Mary should possess what is her Son's. Hence may be inferred how she can free from purgatory the souls of her devotees and fulfil her other promises to the brothers and sisters of the confraternity. For being mother of the Word incarnate, there is due to her a certain power or dominion over all things, spiritual and temporal, to which the authority of her Son extends ; so that she has by natural right of maternity a power almost like that of her Son. Relying, therefore, upon this her participated omnipotency, she promised the devotees of her holy habit (the scapular) to free them from the temporal pains of purgatory, from the eternal pains of hell fire, and from many dangers and calamities of this life, as well spiritual as temporal." Here is part of the religion, here is a portion of the monstrosities of the Carmelites—lay and clerical. The other orders are also implicated ; for scapulars are blessed in Cork, where there are no Carmelites. Mary is their deity, their goddess ; she has imparted to them new revelations, prescribed for them new exercises of devotion, and rendered them perfectly secure of happiness in the world to come. It was through her interposition that the rule of their order or institute was confirmed by Pope Honorius the Third, in the year 1216, when an outcry, for what reason is not mentioned, was raised against their society. It appears that the pope was proceeding too slowly in the matter of confirmation; so much so, that the Virgin, losing all patience, appeared to him in his sleep, and, with severity in her countenance, gave him strict orders to take her devoted children under his special protection, and to confirm the rule of their order—concluding with this threatening expression, " 'Tis not to be contradicted what I command, nor are things to be neglected when I am resolved to promote them." This charge was irresistible. The supineness of the pope was quickened into holy activity; he took the Carmelites under his protection, confirmed without loss of time the rule of their order, and endowed their institute with the most ample privileges. This special apparition and charge of the Virgin to the doubting pope resembles the apparition and language of the angel to St. Joseph, when his mind was in a state of perplexity regarding his betrothed spouse. It is not in one instance that we find true miracles imitated by false ones. The Virgin appeared to Simon Stock times without number, whilst he was sojourning in the cavity of the old oak. She appeared to him subsequently in an especial manner, informing him "that some religious men, who were under her protection, would shortly arrive in England from Palestine, and that he should embrace their institute." These were the Carmelites.

All this was by way of preparing Simon Stock to become one of that holy brotherhood. The prediction, of course, was verified. Two Carmelites, Rodolphus and Yno, came to England from Palestine. Simon waited on them, enrolled himself in their order, and, in a short time, became its distinguished chief.

Her next grand appearance to Simon, who was now commander-in-chief, took place at the delivery of the scapular; on which occasion, having with a multitude of the heavenly host burst into his private oratory at Cambridge, and detailed the principal virtues of the boon she was about to confer, she left the sacred habit in his hands and vanished. This is like a scene in Aladdin. It beggars the fairy tales.

It happened also once upon a time, in the city of Chester, on occasion of a pestilence raging there—a curse that fell on the people in consequence of some disrespect that was shown the Carmelites of that neighbourhood—that a public procession took place to appease the divine wrath. In this procession, however, there happened to be some father Carmelites, who, as the procession moved along, happening to near a wooden statue of the Virgin which was held in the utmost veneration, bowed respectfully to it, saluting it also with the words, "*Ave Maria*,"—"Hail Mary,"—when, lo and behold you, the statue bowed its head respectfully in return. It should rather have curtesied. It also stretched forth a finger, which before was doubled—a strange circumstance in a wooden finger—and, pointing to the father Carmelites in the procession, opened its mouth and distinctly articulated three times the following words:— "Behold these are my brothers." This is a profane imitation of the words addressed by our Saviour when hanging on the cross to his Mother and to John the apostle—"Mother, behold thy Son;" and again, "Son, behold thy Mother." What sacrilegious stuff!!!

Shall we wade any further through this disgusting farrago of falsehood, superstition, and blasphemy? Or shall we still speak of the thousand and one indulgences, plenary and partial, universal and particular, that flow in such abundance from this consecrated bit of patchwork? Or of the privilege it confers on the wearer of extricating kindred souls from purgatory on Wednesdays, as the Virgin is wont to do on Saturdays? We have said more than sufficient for our purpose; that is, that true religion, which must ever repel falsehood and imposture, under every shape and form, can have no connexion whatever with the gross and extravagant superstitions of the scapular.

Nevertheless, this superstition is inculcated in Ireland and elsewhere as a portion of the Roman Catholic religion. Scapulars are worn by a considerable number of silly devotees, who entertain, respecting their virtues, all the extravagancies set down in the scapular book, and consider themselves quite secure of salvation under the hallowed influence of this supernatural amulet. An edition of this book was published a few years ago in Dublin, by the Rev. Mr. Coleman, the provincial of the Carmelites, under the eye, and, of course, with the approbation of the Roman Catholic Archbishop. This edition was got up for the laudable purpose of raising money towards the erection or completion of the then new Carmelite Chapel, in Aungier-street. Doubtless, the wise provincial considered that he was only copying the example of Leo the Tenth, who raised abundance of cash for the building of St. Peter's, by a general sale of indulgences. The new edition of the scapular book was industriously circulated for sale all over the kingdom. The friars, of course, were the chief agents. Every convent was a depôt whence the sacred merchandize, on payment of the needful, was distributed among the people. The bishops and secular clergy looked on in silent acquiescence or approbation. What was this but as far as in them lay to engraft the scapular book on the four gospels; or to identify it with the Roman Catholic religion in Ireland?

But the evil does not rest here. It is not confined to Ireland. It affects the whole church of Rome. The Carmelites, in all matters relating to the scapular, must be supposed to have the sanction and approbation of the Roman See or the Roman Pontiff, the head of the Roman church. He is the liege lord of the Carmelites, and they are his humble vassals. It is he also who has opened what is called the treasure of the church in behalf of the scapular, and enriched it with a countless multitude of indulgences. Here, then, we have the scapular book, and the scapular itself, sanctioned by the highest authority next to that of a general council. But for this fortunate salvo the scapular and its appendages would be an undisputed portion of the Roman Catholic religion ; and the presumptuous essayist, in asserting the contrary, would have committed the audacious and unpardonable crime of heresy. But will this salvo justify the Catholic religion or Catholic church from the reproaches of the Reformers on this score ? If errors and superstitions are inculcated on the minds of the weak and the ignorant, under the full and unqualified sanction of church authority ; under the sanction of generals of orders, of bishops, and of the Roman Pontiff, how can you wipe from the Roman church the stain of contamination, and pretend to exhibit her under such revolting circumstances, without spot or wrinkle, by alleging that no general council gave a solemn decision on the subject ? If the evil be actually mixed up in the mass of Catholicity and solemnly consecrated by those who are looked up to as the propounders and expounders of Roman orthodoxy, the religion of Rome must bear the consequences, and be characterized accordingly—an heterogeneous mixture of good and bad, of truth and falsehood, of religion and superstition.

The superstition of the scapular receives a

sanction even from the Roman Breviary. The 16th of July is a festival in the Roman Calendar, as well as in that of the Carmelites. It is called the feast of the blessed Mary of Mount Carmel. The lessons of the second *nocturn* contain nearly the sum and substance of the scapular book itself. We there find honorable mention made of Simon Stock; how he received the *holy scapular* from the hands of the Virgin, as the distinguished badge of the Carmelite order, and as a safeguard and protection in the hour of danger; also, that the Virgin appeared to Pope Honorius the Third, charging him strictly to take the Carmelites collectively and individually under his protection; and lastly, that the Virgin is pledged to release the devout of the scapular, without loss of time, from the fiery prison of purgatory.* From this it is manifest, that his Grace the Most Rev. Dr. Murray could not well refuse his "*inprimatur*" to the scapular book; unless, indeed, he ventured to exercise a similar authority over the Roman Breviary, with which it is quite in keeping—a thing not to be expected in these times of caution and expediency. The scapular, therefore, seems to be propped up by all the weight of ecclesiastical and religious authority: by the authority of the Carmelites, who are its professed abettors; by the authority of the Pope, who is the grand master of the Carmelite order, and of

* Vide Roman Breviary, 16th July.

all the orders; by the authority of the episcopal body, who all act in subordination to the Pope; and finally, by the authority of that volume, the Roman Breviary, which the secular clergy are bound daily to peruse, under the penalty of mortal sin, or hell-fire.

Now, under all these circumstances, we ask seriously, have not the Reformers made out a case; and are not they warranted in saying, that the Roman Catholic church permits religion to be outraged by the grossest absurdities and superstitions? What can be said at the opposite side? What defence can be set up?

The Gallican church does not recognize the scapular. But this church is considered by the ultramontanists, as half schismatic. The student for holy orders learns nothing in the course of his studies respecting the scapular; it forms no part of his theology. Neither Bellarmine, nor Tournelli, nor Bailly, nor De la Hogue, has said or written a word on the subject. It is only after quitting college, and when the tyro priest enters upon the duties of his ministry, that he begins to learn something of the scapular and its extraordinary virtues. What is mentioned in the Breviary lessons for the 16th of July, might, indeed, arrest his attention a little in college; but he learns nothing of any consequence on the subject until he comes in business-like collision with the interested high priests of the scapular, and its deluded votaries. He sees, with surprise, this morbid extension of religion. But he finds himself so circumstanced, that he cannot, without incurring the guilt of heresy, attempt to denounce such a state of things. He copies the example of his more experienced brethren, holds his peace like a wise man, and acquiesces in the unhallowed intermixture.

Further, no authorized catechism contains a syllable about the scapular. Children are instructed in the mysteries of religion, in the decalogue, the precepts of the church, the nature of prayer, the sacraments, and respecting the final state of mankind. But they receive not a word of instruction respecting the scapular, as if it had no connection whatever with religion. The secular clergy never make it the subject of their sermons or public exhortations ; there is no mention made of it in the common prayer books, or the books of devotion published for the use of the laity. Why is the scapular thus dishonored or laid aside ? Why, also, in the various treatises on theology, is not a chapter devoted to Simon Stock and the blessed scapular ? Why do they not form an important item in some body of divinity ? Why are catechisms, why are all the books of devotion, why are preachers, why are the accredited instructors of the people ever silent on the subject ? Why such heedlessness, such neglect, such profound taciturnity in a matter involving the religious devotions and exercises of so large a body of the faithful ?

Ye bishops and priests, who call yourselves the apostles of infallibility, and pretend that you never teach, or sanction, or overlook anything erroneous or immoral, declare the truth in this important matter. Do you give credence to the revelations of Simon Stock, and to the miraculous virtues of the scapular ? Or are you not, on the contrary, fully aware of their falsehood, their profaneness, their ridiculousness, and their absurdity ? Yes, this must of necessity be the case ; and therefore it is, that ye remain silent, and keep, as it were, aloof from these vile and disgusting excrescences of religion, from scapulars, and habits, and other consecrated trumpery. But do you imagine that your silence, under such circumstances, can be justified ? Are ye not called on, by the principles ye avow, and the functions ye have undertaken to discharge, to take active and effectual steps to remedy this crying evil—to separate truth from falsehood, and to rescue religion from the fangs of superstition ? Your flocks are the dupes of interested craft and imposture ; and you look on with silent apathy and indifference. You leave them to learn their duty to the God of truth from the apostles of falsehood. Ye see it, ye know it, ye connive at it, ye sanction it, as ye did the impostures of Hohenlohe ; yea, more, ye are, by your intimate connexion with the regulars, fully incorporated with the entire system of superstition and fraud.

Degenerate priests of the new covenant ; pseudo

oracles of infallibility; children of sacrilegious expediency; time-servers in religion and politics; imitators of the philosophers of old, who declared the truth of God in unrighteousness, go, substitute the scapular book for the gospel, and Simon Stock for Jesus Christ.

CHAPTER XXIX.

A DIGRESSION TO A COGNATE SUBJECT.

"I am certainly persuaded that all our misfortunes arise from no other original cause than that general disregard among us for the public welfare."—SWIFT'S SERMON ON DOING GOOD.

THE Roman Catholic Clergy of Ireland have laid themselves open to many objections on the score of religion and politics. It is their duty to instruct by word and by example, and to render the people, if possible, moral and religious; to make them good Christians, and good members of society. The question is, are they discharging this obligation, or are they acting a contrary part? In days gone by the priests of Ireland meddled not with politics; but perhaps they deserve no credit on that account, for the circumstances of the time forbade all such interference. Their attention, therefore, should be supposed to have been entirely directed to the religious and moral improvement of the people. But did they in reality exercise a salutary influence in this respect? This question cannot be answered unqualifiedly in the affirmative. If they ever exercised an influence of this description, why did it not appear in the improved morals of the people? Why did family feuds continue in full force? Why were their flocks cut up into factions, breathing continually the malignant spirit of mutual hostility and vengeance? And why was this spirit transmitted from generation to generation? If their flocks, or the descendants of their flocks have become somewhat improved in this respect; if less blood be now shed in family quarrels; if rival factions, belonging to the same neighbourhood, and to the same religious persuasion, appear in battle array less frequently than in former times—is this improvement attributable to priestly influence or to the operation of law? One thing is certain, that when once the common people set the law at defiance, they plunge into the greatest excesses—regardless of any other control or authority.

Terror is the talisman by which the Irish priests were wont to maintain their influence over the illiterate multitude. Nothing, in former times, was more frequent than solemn curses and excommunications, more especially in wild and savage districts; for these terrific denunciations are generally in a direct ratio with ignorance and incivilization.

The ideas of the multitude have not undergone much alteration for the better in this particular. Many still stand in awe of the priest's curse ; who, they fancy, can, by the exercise of preternatural power, sicken their cattle, blight their corn, and cause, at will, the vial of God's wrath to be poured down upon the world. This ridiculous fancy or persuasion contributes to uphold the influence of the priest. But this is a malevolent influence—an influence arising from a frightful compound or combination of jugglery, imposture and superstition. Priestly influence, particularly in times past, however it might have furnished matter for commendation, very much resembled that of necromancers or magicians. Good men, especially public functionaries, must, of necessity, possess considerable influence ; and, doubtless, the Irish Catholic priesthood have furnished characters of this description. This, however, is an influence, "*per accidens*," arising not so much from the functions of the priest as from the virtues of the individual. But let us look exactly into the present state of things in this respect.

What have the Irish Catholic bishops and priests done of late years to improve the morals of the people and to make them better Christians ? What example have they themselves exhibited ? Let us begin with the celebrated Dr. James Doyle, who is now no more, but whose works and doctrines live, and are in active operation. This man, who was a professor of theology for some time in the seminary of Carlow, commenced, after he became a bishop, a new course of ethics, for the benefit of his flock. He preached the doctrine of resistance to law, as far as regarded church property; and made it, in a great measure, a matter of conscience to reduce this doctrine to practice. The priests of his own diocess, as might be expected, embraced the doctrine of their bishop, and preached it to their flocks. The contagion spread, like a pestilence, through the country. In all quarters, resistance to law was inculcated, and practised, too, with a vengeance; and the authority of Dr. Doyle was quoted in justification. The Irish Catholic episcopal body have either positively or negatively acquiesced in all this; so that the doctrine of "resistance to law," as regards church property, has become part of the moral code of Roman Catholic Ireland. Indeed so much is this the case, that whoever holds a different opinion, or does not act in conformity with the Doylite theology, or with this antinomian system, is considered a heretic, or a favourer of heresy, and is marked out accordingly for persecution. This was the head and front of the author's offending, and the great cause why, at last, after a long series of annoyances, he was deprived of his benefice, and made to suffer all the evils of clerical and episcopal vengeance.

To this perversion of the moral code may be ascribed the horrible murders and outrages of every description that have become, this time past, so common in this unhappy country. These cruelties are, indeed, considered as the necessary means for the accomplishment of a consecrated object—the subversion of the Protestant establishment; and the priests themselves do not scruple, if not to justify, at least to palliate their perpetration. When lives are sacrificed upon these lawless occasions, these ministers of religion observe with an inhuman "*sang froid*," that the good proposed cannot be obtained but by sacrifices of the kind—that this is the natural course of things.

This modern antinomianism produces two great evils. It compromises the duty of civil allegiance, which the Catholic church in former times inculcated, and it establishes principles subversive of all contracts and covenants between man and man. For whatever may be said of the abstract nature of tithes, the obligation of their payment rests upon the fact that an equivalent is received—namely, the land, which is to all intents and purposes the set-off, as well against the dues of the church, as the rent of the landlord.

But let us say a few words more about Dr. Doyle, who, indeed, enacted a strange part in religion and politics. At one time he volunteered to proclaim,—and his proclamation made much noise,—that the two rival churches of England and Rome may, without much difficulty, be reconciled; that the points of difference were not many, and by no means essential. And yet shortly after, when it was proposed to examine and argue the controverted points, this same liberal and enlightened Doctor issued a pastoral, prohibiting, within his diocess, all discussion of the kind—declaring, at the same time, that all sectaries, without exception, were bound to submit, unconditionally, to the definitions and authority of the Roman Catholic church. This was consistency with a vengeance. Great geniuses, it is said, are apt to run into opposite extremes.

There was a time also when he expressed himself satisfied with the tithe composition act. But soon after nothing would satisfy him short of the total abolition of tithes, under every shape and form. The reason he assigned for this change in his sentiments is odd enough—namely, that the Protestant clergy, indeed, in the intermediate period, had abused the Catholic religion. What was this but to be actuated by mere spite and vindictiveness?—motives utterly unworthy of a great man.

> Tantœne animis cælestibus iræ.
> Can heavenly minds such high resentment show,
> And exercise their spite in human woe?—DRYDEN.

He eulogized a certain poor ignorant man, who took a copy of the Bible or New Testament up with a tongs—not wishing to contaminate his fingers by touching it—and laid it with all due form in a grave dug for that curious purpose. It is hard to say which displayed the worse taste, the man who entombed the Sacred Volume, or the bishop who applauded the act. The poor man, of course, acted through blindness, which was rendered incurable by the extravagant encomium of the bishop.

If the doctrine he lays down on the law of prescription be correct, there is scarcely a proprietor in Ireland who possesses a just title to his land; centuries of possession or occupancy will not validate the rights of the present legal owners. This doctrine is directly opposed to the peace of the community and to the stability of society. The first possessor had a bad title, and this radical fault could not be cured by any length of possession. This is his reasoning on property tenures by prescription, or by the right of conquest. It may be asked, in regard to those who were deprived formerly of their properties by the fortune of war, upon what foundation did they rest their title? No doubt their titles rested also upon forcible or unjust occupancy at the beginning; that their right was founded in might, according to the maxim of Hobbes. Perhaps even church property, which gave so much uneasiness to the Doctor, was originally an unjustifiable appropriation made by the hand of power; in which case, from his own shewing, the present claimants or possessors have just as good a title to it as the old Irish church had, previous to the Reformation. But let us quit the individual and speak of the Irish Catholic episcopal body in general, in reference to the subject in hand.

In times gone by, when some relaxation of the

penal laws or popery code took place, a large proportion of it still remaining on the statute book, the Irish Catholic bishops made great demonstrations of loyalty. The leading prelates of the time were Butler of Cashel, Troy of Dublin, Moylan of Cork, and Plunket of Meath. All their pastoral letters, and they were not niggardly in issuing them, breathed sentiments of the purest loyalty and allegiance, and teemed with expressions of respect for the constituted authorities. All this was put forth, too, as necessarily dictated by the genuine principles of Roman orthodoxy. Solemn prayers were, for a considerable period, regularly offered up at the public service for the king and royal family. The *Domine salvum fac regem*, or God save the king, was sung at the solemn high mass. Even the formidable conspiracy of united Irishmen, which threatened the overthrow of British dominion in Ireland, was denounced by them as opposed to every law, human and divine. All these demonstrations of loyalty and obedience furnished the advocates for Catholic emancipation with powerful arguments in favour of that long disputed measure, and to a great extent disarmed its opponents; who, indeed, rested their objections upon supposed Catholic principles, which were believed to be on record and to continue unchanged and unchangeable in conformity with the professed nature or genius of the Catholic religion. Dr. Troy, and other bishops and divines, wrote pamphlets on this all-engrossing subject, in which obedience to law and respect for the constituted authorities were uniformly inculcated, as an indispensable duty—a duty not of occasional expediency, but of absolute obligation. How different all this from the conduct of the Irish Catholic prelates of the present day; when the very religion, of which these dignitaries are the rulers or administrators, is identified with resistance to law and contempt for the constituted authorities; and all this, too, when relieved from the galling incubus of the penal code, this same Catholic religion is left unfettered and free.

What conclusion is to be drawn from all this? Does the Catholic church, or the Catholic religion, now proclaim its true principles? And were all the demonstrations formerly made hypocritical and false? Is the language of the Irish Catholic hierarchy mere political jargon, masked by pretended religion, and put forth to answer a present purpose? Were the old bishops sincere, or were they not? Let us attend to facts.

In the hey-day of expectation nothing but glowing testimonies of loyalty and liberality. During that fleeting period, prayers for the king and royal family and for the success of his arms, were constantly incorporated with the public service of the church. This fit of loyal devotion was too intense to be lasting. Disappointed hopes damped its ardour and produced a counteraction. The holy effusions of loyalty greeted less frequently the ears of the congregation, gradually fell into disuse, and, after a time, were heard no more. The king, and the queen consort, and the royal family, were struck out of the dyptics, and the success of the royal arms was left to chance and the fortune of war. This was no great proof of sincerity. On the contrary, it would appear that they acted all along as politicians or as hypocrites, as far as religion was concerned. But there is another circumstance, not to be omitted, that subjects them, in a more tangible manner, to this latter charge—namely, that at no period, even in the full effervescence of their loyalty, did they mention the king's name in the canon of the mass—that is, in the particular part of the solemn service where, according to the general rubricks, his name should of right be associated with that of the pope and of the ordinary of the particular diocess. The rubrick was made a dead letter, because of the heterodoxy of the monarch. This, however, was kept a secret. We now ask, why were prayers for the monarch incorporated at all with the church service, if such incorporation was contrary to the usages of the Catholic church? And if to do so was in conformity with these usages, why was he not prayed for at the time and in the manner prescribed by the Roman ritual? Was not all this a delusion practised on the people?—who, for a time, had reason to be persuaded, that prayers for their king, &c. &c., formed part of their liturgy, and were consequently thenceforward to be included within the range of their own religious exercises. They never dreamed of the unhallowed contrast between the solemn public exhibition of religious loyalty towards George the Third and the royal family, and the silent but pointed rejection of his name from the canon of the mass, or the *sanctum sanctorum* of the church service.

Candour and straightforwardness have not been this long time the characteristics of these successors to the Apostles. They have uniformly succumbed, as we have said elsewhere, to the strength of popular prejudices or to the violence of faction. At the period of the Legislative Union, they thought it not inconsistent with the principles or welfare of the Catholic religion, to accept the "*regium donum*," if offered; and to vest in the crown a veto on their particular appointments. Soon after, however, they publicly proclaimed the inexpediency of any such *concordatum*. The matter did not stop here. Pursuing the same deflecting course, they made, after another short lapse of time, an announcement "*ex cathedra*," that the concession of any royal veto would necessarily lead to the subversion of the Roman Catholic religion in Ireland. This may be denominated the march of episcopal intellect, much resembling the movement of the moon and planets relatively to the sun; from conjunction to quadratures, and from quadratures to opposition. Will they stand firm in the present position they have taken? or will they pursue a counter track? or a course of retrogradation? Will they return to the point whence they started, and enter once more into friendly conjunction with the powers that be? A little time may clear up this matter. But what practical conclusion should be come to with respect to these same right reverend gentlemen? Ought the people to bow to their authority, or copy their example? They endeavour to persuade the multitude that they act by the impulse of heaven, notwithstanding their unsteadiness, their duplicity, and their inconsistencies. But let them declare the truth, and acknowledge, by way of reparation, that they have been influenced from the outset, not by the spirit of truth, which abhors deceit, nor by any consideration arising from the merits of the subject, or indeed from any sense of religious or moral obligation, but by motives of interest, by feelings of disappointment, by national antipathies, sectarian prejudices, and popular intimidation; in a word, by all those extraordinary springs of action, that strangely diversify human occurrences, and give new and contradictory combinations to the elements of human society.

The strange and inconsistent conduct of the bishops and priests, has produced its natural effect upon the laity, who, indeed, are puzzled and perplexed, both as to religion and politics. The conduct of the priests, in respect to tithes, has given scandal even to those who took an active part in the proceedings. It is a common remark that priests, far from taking a lead, should have kept aloof; that it did not become persons of their calling to appear at the head of tumultuous assemblies, and to lend their assistance in the dangerous work of popular excitement. Persons, in the lowest rank of the community, have reasoned after this manner, and they frequently express their astonishment, that they were exhorted by the ministers of religion to expose themselves to the many dangers that must attend a systematic opposition to government and law.

It may be curious here to remark, that some priests attempt to justify their conduct by saying, that they should go with, what they call, the people, as if they were warranted in compromising the duties of their ministry ; and, instead of leading, suffer themselves to be led ; while, on the other hand, the deluded people affirm that they never would have proceeded to such extremities but for the example and instruction of the priests. The difference between these conflicting statements is, that the latter is correct ; so that the charge of misrepresentation lies at the door of the former, to say nothing of the compromise of principle, of which, from their own showing, they stand convicted. The whole matter, if we credit both sides, may be stated thus : The flocks were led astray by the pastors, and the pastors (poor gentlemen) were led astray by their flocks.

But let us suppose, that through terror or a sense of expediency, the priests consented to travel in the wake of the multitude ; how does such a humiliating position square with Catholic principles? How squares it with church authority, which exercises such high prerogatives; or with church infallibility, that hushes to silence all profane gainsayers? Have things, then, come to that sorry pass, that churchmen have dwindled into the insignificance of unlettered laymen; and, like other obscure individuals, must, no matter for what purpose or object, swell the numbers of the ignoble multitude? Yes, such, alas! is the case in this our island of saints. "Tell it not in Gath—tell it not in Ascalon, lest the daughters of the Philistine rejoice."

But do they speak the truth when they say, they went with their flocks? Have they gone with the aristocracy of their communion, a class that never identified themselves with resistance to law? We may put a similar question respecting a considerable number of the middle orders; and give it a similar answer. We also know that many who were in the habit of assembling and combining, acted thus under the influence of terror and intimidation. Did the priests even go with this portion of their flocks? We think not exactly. But, taking these three classes into consideration, what is the meaning of the fine phrase "going with the people?" They have abandoned the manly, the enlightened, the well-disposed, and attached themselves to the desperadoes of the community. Still they exclaim, "we go with the people." Together with being bad philosophers, and bad theologians, they have become very licentious rhetoricians; for they make a very improper use of the figure synechdoche, which puts *pars pro toto*, a portion for the entire. They have ventured to swell the least worthy portion of their congregations into the imposing consequence of totality, and that, too, for the selfish purpose of covering their own ignominy.

The priests have injured their own character and that of their religion. They can no longer be viewed in the light of ministers of the gospel, but as the tools of faction. No more can be applied to them the saying of holy writ, "How beautiful are the feet of those who bring tidings of good things: who bring tidings of peace." They are no longer what they ought to be, the heralds of peace and conciliation, but the arch-fomentors of bigotry and civil discord, of lawlessness and sedition. The people are every where reasoning and reflecting on the subject, and drawing their conclusions. The age of blind obedience is passing away; the priests themselves have broken the spell, nor will the "*ipse dixit*" of a churchman, though robed in his vestments, any longer pass as a divine oracle. The eyes of all have, in a great measure, been opened by the extraordinary and unprecedented scenes that have been exhibited this time past, and a revolution or reformation in religion seems fast approaching in this country.

The multitude, indeed, are kept together for the present by a variety of causes: by the force of habit, by the spirit of party, and by the dread of singularity. Lutherans, and Calvinists, and Roman Catholics, were all mingled together for a considerable time at the commencement of the Reformation. But the jarring elements that were brought into permanent and increasing operation, soon produced their natural effects ; and the great ancient religious or superstitious community was broken up into various conflicting sects and divisions. To compare great things with small, the Catholics of Ireland, as they are called, (for the term itself has now no other meaning but that of a party appellation,) have anything among them but unity and uniformity, properly speaking. The mass, indeed, is still celebrated, and the usual number of sacraments occasionally administered. These things are kept up as matters of course by the priests, and are acquiesced in by the people. But as to religious dogmata or opinions : as to the deference that should be paid to the clergy, or the ideas that are entertained respecting the particular merits of the Roman Catholic religion or church, nothing but discord and contrariety. A considerable number of the better order, who go under the name of Catholics, have an utter disregard for their priests, and for the doctrines they teach ; seldom go to mass ; never to confession ; do not believe the ghostly fathers to be unerring guides in religion ; nor that the salvation or damnation of souls depends upon the capricious or interested interference of such questionable characters.

The common people are placed in a dilemma of a very unsatisfactory and dangerous description. From the anti-religious conduct, and carriage, and preaching of their priests, they are at a loss to determine what is right and what is wrong. They have worked themselves into the belief that anti-tithe combination is a holy war; and many consider that all means may be used to effectuate their purpose. It was this dreadful impression, produced by priestly interference, that caused them for the moment, in opposition to every law, human and divine, to set little value on the lives of their fellow creatures, and made them imagine that to perpetrate murder was to perform an act of justice. This class of persons, however, notwithstanding all the pains that have been taken to pervert them, have their doubts and misgivings, and do feel, on cool reflection, great surprise, that religion should be made to preach any thing but peace and good will to mankind. In short, the moderate and reflecting portion of the Catholic body altogether are filled with doubts and difficulties as to religion and its ministers, owing chiefly to the systematic scenes of lawless extravagance exhibited by the latter, since their enlistment under the tumultuous banner of faction and agitation.

This portion of the community may, indeed, covet the abolition of tithes, and the subversion of the church establishment, which latter is the principal object aimed at ; but they look with dismay at the means employed for its accomplishment ; and are shocked that the religion they were taught to venerate, should be made ancillary to injury and outrage. The priests have sunk in their estimation ; and, as invariably happens, the religion itself, sharing the fate of its ministers, must cease to command their respect. Thus from a heterogeneous combination of infidelity, and scepticism, and mistrust, and scandal, and the dissemination of bad principles of action, and the anti-religious position of their clergy, the Roman Catholic body of Ireland, notwithstanding the swaggering encomiums of political spouters, is an anomalous compound, having within it all the seeds of schism, strife, and dismemberment.

They are equally bewildered as to politics. Every thing possible has been done by interested persons to bring even the meanest of the people on the political arena, and to press them into the service of faction. The ghostly gentry, too, have been the principal agents in this extraordinary business. The peasantry, instead of the gospel, have had to listen in their houses of worship to discussions on abstract questions of legislation and political economy, by persons ill-qualified for the task, but whom no one dare to contradict. The most ridiculous notions are crammed down the throats of those who cannot comprehend their meaning or tendency. The poor ignorant people are wound up, like puppets or automata, to utter in unison certain words or phrases of mighty import and signification ; and this is denominated " public opinion."

Let us come to particulars :

Politicians of a certain description are to be sent into parliament, the followers of the great and mighty Dan. This batch seated in the senate-house are to carry all before them, to make the hated Saxon quail, to be so many political Hohenlohes, to work in double quick time the redemption of the country, to abolish tithes, annihilate the church establishment, overthrow corporations, humble the aristocracy, and by the repeal of the union, insure for ever the independence of Ireland. The priests, the ministers of the gospel, in obedience to their liege lord and for the public good, undertake to forward this important business; and pressing religion into the service, make it a matter of conscience with their abused congregations, to vote according to their holy directions. Reckless of consequences, they interpose between the tenant and his landlord, and endeavour, from the altar, at the time of mass, to persuade the poor man that if he does not place himself in hostility with the lord of the soil, to his own great detriment and that of his poor family, he will violate the most sacred of duties, and run the imminent risk of eternal damnation. In this manner do the priests endeavour to execute their task of popular perversion and ruin.

The poor people are made the dupes of every species of imposition, religious and political.

This novel mode of predication has produced a corresponding effect. The lowest class of the community, cow-boys, churn-boys, handy-craft men of the lowest grade, labourers, and small farmers, are metamorphosed into busy, brawling, impertinent, pragmatical politicians, like as happened in the days of Cromwell, when—

> The oyster women lock'd their fish up,
> And trugged away to cry "no Bishop."
>
> HUDIBRASS.

What extraordinary personages are those priests, notwithstanding the profusion to be found among them of meanness and ignorance. They prove to the world that the power they possess, passing by spirituals, operates at once on the elements of inert matter and in the elements of civil society.

But how does the Irish Roman Catholic body, taken as a whole, stand in regard to politics? What is their position in this respect? The faction, of which the priests are the pioneers, and of which the lower order constitutes the strength, appear to be all-powerful among them. But, first of all, are the poor people satisfied that their spiritual directors have given them sound advice; and that there is wisdom and good policy in their opposing themselves to their landlords, and that, too,—making the most favourable supposition—in a matter of contingent or conjectural good? Many of them have seen things from the beginning in the true light, but they have been afraid to act in conformity to their opinions. They dread the curse of the priest and the savage hostility of their neighbours. Some of them were driven to register their supposed franchise contrary to their consciences. Unable to pay their rents, they scrupled, and not without reason, to swear to a ten-pound interest in their holding. But the consecrated demagogue overruled their scruples, and insisted, at all hazards, on their taking out the necessary qualification. Religion, and conscience, and truth, and prudence, have been sacrificed on the altar of political faction and intrigue. But the minds of the poor people are by no means easy upon this matter; on the contrary, what with their own lack of knowledge and the terrors of their church, and their private interests, and the confusion of contradictory opinions, they are involved in great doubt and perplexity; so that the oracular infallibility of their spiritual and now political directors is, even in regard to these, their humble children, tottering on its base.

As you ascend in the scale of society the clashing of politics is marked and defined. The great leader—the most outrageous political demagogue of modern times—is followed by a numerous and uproarious squad—handy-craft men, conceited clerks, small shopkeepers, struggling merchants, obscure attorneys, briefless barristers, and some would-be squireens. This motley group are the common disturbers of the whole country; and, though possessing a sort of unity as to party and faction, contain within themselves the active elements of discord and confusion. They seem to have nothing definite or determinate in view—ever unsteady, ever changing, never satisfied. As to their chief, he has gone round all the points of the political compass, and has somehow contrived to drag them after him—vetoists and anti-vetoists; against the *regium donum*, for the *regium donum;* in favour of poor laws, against poor laws; reform, the great panacea; then repeal, the great panacea; calling for a restriction of the elective franchise, and for an extension of the elective franchise; shouting for liberty, yet imposing the most galling slavery; professing liberality, yet fostering bigotry; preaching obedience to law, yet inculcating resistance to it as a duty of paramount obligation; acknowledging that the Protestant clergy ought to be supported, yet moving heaven and hell to reduce them to a state of starvation; reprobating clerical interference in politics, then turning round and reprobating any clergyman who keeps aloof from politics—a faction, in short, exhibiting in themselves, head and members, all the wayward extravagancies of political inconsistency.

The seceders from these turbulent and unprincipled spirits are denounced as apostates to their religion and traitors to their country; and are held up as proper objects of public hatred and persecution. Their sway has been terrific this time past. But the period of terror is passing away, notwithstanding all the efforts of the priests to prolong it. A re-action is in progress. Some of the very leading actors in the scene, disgusted with what they saw and the position they were made to occupy, have turned round upon their associates and taskmasters, pourtrayed in the blackest colours the arch-fiend of agitation, and, in the face of the world, renounced all his works and pomps.

Public virtue is nearly out of the question these extraordinary times, and party spirit constitutes the order of the day. It is all the same in this respect with the priest and with the flock. "All have gone astray, all have become unprofitable together." Several of the priesthood and the episcopal body lament the present novel and unhappy state of Irish society, but take good care not to give publicity to their sentiments. On the contrary, they acquiesce in the popular delusion; or, like the consecrators of the scapular, they applaud in public what they reprobate in private. Is this public virtue?—to say nothing of their dereliction of duty as Christian bishops. And what course were they bound to pursue? Was it not incumbent on them, were they not called upon "*ex-officio*," to issue pastoral letters enjoining, as an indispensable duty, submission to the laws and respect for the constituted authorities, as was done formerly by Dr. Troy and the bishops of the time, under similar circumstances, agreeably to the maxims of the gospel and to the avowed principles of the Roman Catholic church? It is quite certain, whatever may be said of the episcopal body in general, that some individuals among them feel that this line of conduct should have been pursued; and yet acted on by the force of popular excitement and the new-fangled ideas of their brethren, they shrunk from the performance of their duty, and either by criminal silence or by criminal interference, by connivance or positive approval, have assisted in furthering the unhallowed work of insubordination and outrage. The probability is, that this charge comes home in a more or less degree to every individual of this body—not excepting Dr. Doyle himself, the great *primum mobile* of anti-tithe agitation. For it appears that this same doctor, rightly indeed enough, but with strange inconsistency, objected to have put in nomination for the then vacant see of Cloyne, the Rev. John O'Connell, now parish priest of Mitchelstown, for no other reason but that he took so leading a part in the anti-tithe war. But to pursue our subject. Scarcely a bishop has shewn a particle of public virtue; but collectively and individually have either fomented or acquiesced in the popular delusion.

Among the clergy of the second order there were a few exceptions—a solitary example here and there of unbending integrity and virtue.

> Apparent rari nantes in gurgite vasto.
> But few, alas, the raging waves withstood,
> The multitude were buried in the flood.

These honorable exceptions had to contend with difficulties of no ordinary description ; with a merciless faction, with a maddened multitude, with the shameless hostility of their own brethren or order, and the frowns of their mitred superiors. They were examples of the steady, upright man described by Horace, who is not scared from his purpose by the frowns of the tyrant, or by the fury of the populace,

> Justum et tenacem propositi virum,
> Non arder civium prava jubentium,
> Non vultus instantis tyranni,
> Mente quatit solida.
> The man resolved and steady to his trust,
> Inflexible to ill and obstinately just,
> May the rude rabble's insolence despise,
> Their senseless clamours and tumultuous cries.
> The tyrant's fierceness he beguiles,
> And the stern brow and the hoarse defies,
> And with superior greatness smiles.—Addison.

They were vilified, they were calumniated, they were loaded with obloquy; they were denounced as foes to the people, and as hirelings of a tyrannical government. Their houses were threatened, their lives were threatened, their authority was subverted, and their chapels were closed against them. "*Secti sunt, lapidati sunt*"—"they were sawed asunder, they were stoned." Priests and people were leagued together for their destruction. But they endured every thing, braved every thing, risked every thing ; in a word, they suffered civil martyrdom for the great cause of religion and social order. They were gifted with a divine energy to which the episcopal body and the great mass of their own order were strangers; and this energy rendered them unconquerable.

> Pauci quos æquus amavit
> Jupiter, aut ardens evexit ad sidera vertus
> Dis geniti potuere.
>
> To few great Jupiter imparts this grace,
> And those of shining worth and heavenly race.

Yes, their number is small, and not worthy to be taken into account in our estimate of the times, which must be characterised, not by the virtues of the scanty few, but by the absence of virtue in the multitude. Let us now pass to the laity. How do they stand in reference to public virtue?

There is an unlucky coincidence in this particular—a melancholy reciprocity of guilt. We speak not here of the giddy crowd, who are little better than machines set in motion by a sort of master-puppets, to produce certain effects, as occasion may require. With these latter we have to do—namely, our busy, active, leading politicians, who would fain get into their hands the management of public affairs, and who boast of being the regenerators of unhappy Ireland. Of what description are these for the most part? Do they abound in public virtue? We have limbs of the law, who labour in this cause for the purpose of bringing themelves into notoriety and advancing themselves in their profession. Several of them, too, have gained more substantial rewards for their noisy patriotism. The Catholic rent, in its time, which was so much spoil or wages judiciously divided among them, must have proved a mighty stimulus. It is easy to account for the part these good folk have acted without having recourse to public virtue. They have merely acted the parts assigned them, or which they were permitted to assume, in the general drama. Some are newspaper editors or political writers, who, with an utter disregard of principle, or the public welfare, cater merely to party taste, for their own private interest or that of their establishment. We speak of individuals.

This consideration of self-interest, which is directly opposed to public virtue, converted into flaming patriots many persons in trade, who very readily came to the conclusion that their success in business might depend, in a great measure, on their pandering to prevailing prejudices. Are we, said they, to lose our customers and injure our families, or let slip an opportunity of making our fortune? What a large share of public virtue is possessed by gentry of this description!

The sham and adventurous patriotism of individuals had an effect like magic upon all those of the same caste. All followed the example of the leaders, as well to defeat the unprincipled speculations of individuals as to sustain themselves. The patriotism of all these is a compound of envy, jealousy, selfishness, and cupidity. We pass by in silence the monopolizing spirit of the great leader of the whole gang.

A great point, indeed the main point, with all these flaming patriots is, by all means, to keep up the popular excitement—well knowing that this is the state of things in which alone they can "live, and move, and have their being." For this purpose new questions are started, which, however impracticable, produce the intended effect—that is, to fill the multitude with extravagant hopes and expectations. The repeal of the union is a question of this description. It is acknowledged that the first cry for repeal was a mere ruse; that the accomplishment of that measure was not contemplated by those who first disturbed the nation on the subject; and who, notwithstanding, laboured might and main to propagate the idea that it was the only panacea for existing evils, and was absolutely necessary for the prosperity of the country. What was this but political jugglery and double-dealing? The great agitator himself, perhaps unwittingly, let out the secret. The agitation for repeal was at the out-set only a means to accomplish, of course, something else. Afterwards repeal itself became the end proposed. New light broke in upon the gentleman; the political mask which cloaked the question at the commencement was thrown aside, and the avowed object, after considerable delay and uproar, became the real one. Can the prime actors in this varying equivocal scene claim to themselves any portion of public virtue?

It is a question if the new language they adopted was the language of sincerity; for they have thought proper at present to place their favourite measure in abeyance. But let us view the thing itself in a practical light. Is the great Liberator of opinion, that the repeal of the union can be accomplished? That it is a practicable measure? Or has he raised the question from some sinister or interested motive? Has he taken it up as one best adapted to prolong the period of civil agitation and to establish for himself a permanent claim to the contributions of the silly multitude? Does he seek in all this the public good or his own private emolument?

There are but two ways of determining the question of repeal—namely, either in parliament or in the field; either by civil deliberation or by civil convulsion. Does he feed himself up with the fancy that he will carry the measure in the former way—that is, through the Imperial Parliament? That a measure supported by a contemptible section of the house, at odds too with themselves on the subject; and opposed by the united interest of England, Scotland, and Ireland, as fraught with danger to the empire at large, is likely to receive the deliberate sanction of the three estates of the realm—the King, the Lords, and the Commons? That a law, enacted to ensure the connection between Ireland and England, and to consolidate the whole empire : a law considered fundamental and irrevocable to all intents and purposes, and upon the supposed permanence of which the Imperial Parliament has proceeded in its career of legislation, now for upwards of thirty years : that a law of this all-important description will be repealed at the instance of a faction that breathes nothing but threatenings and slaughter, civil anarchy, civil tumult, and civil dismemberment ? But if his object is to have recourse to the other alternative, as his language often indicates ; if his object is to embroil the empire in the calamities of civil war, for the accomplishment of that which, under the most favourable supposition, is only a contingent or problematical good, then is he nothing more or less than a political desperado, seeking to cause a new deluge of evils to overflow his unhappy country. Are his followers and admirers prepared to go with him to all these extremities ? Or can it be supposed that the man entertains so wicked and so chimerical a project ? But if upon a view of the whole case, he neither can hope to carry the measure through Parliament ; nor, on the other hand, entertain the wish of making the bloody and hazardous experiment of carrying it by the sword, what light are we to view him in but that of an arch political impostor, wholly employed in deluding a credulous people with vain projects and expectations, and placing, for the basest purposes, every possible bar to social improvement, and to the public welfare ?

What are we to think of these public men who form the tail of this great leviathan ? Have they among them a large portion of public virtue ?—these great optimists in legislation, who propose to regenerate the empire, and restore the golden age on earth. Methinks it requires no great process of reasoning to come to a conclusion on this point. If the master they serve be deficient in public virtue, we cannot suppose it to abound in them. The truth is, that these exalted personages have no will or opinion of their own. They are, in every sense of the word, slaves to an individual, to whom they owe their political existence, and to the multitude who are guided by that same individual. They must obey the leader inside the house, and the sovereign people outside. They have, indeed, divested themselves of the privilege of rational beings, and become mere political automata. The Coercion Bill had well nigh broken the spell, or, to use a vulgar phrase, let the cat out of the bag. Opposition was given to it by those who were convinced of its necessity. But another necessity, which it is unnecessary to specify, overruled every consideration for the public welfare. This was public virtue with a vengeance.

Some of these sublime personages are known to hold their leader in utter detestation, and to disapprove of the system he is pursuing. They even at times make indirect attacks on him through the press, and are attacked by him in turn ; or rather, he commences the assault, and they make some puny effort at retaliation. But manly, virtuous opposition, is out of the question. They succumb again, hug the yoke of servility, and embrace the knees of their lord and master. What is this but the essence of political depravity, or the total absence of public virtue? The leader, his satellites, the bishops, the priests, professional men, and men in business, all leagued together to the great disturbance and evil of society, in a shameless confederacy of tyranny, slavery, injustice, profanation, imposition, selfishness, double-dealing, and hypocrisy.

CHAPTER XXX.

OF RELIGIOUS INTOLERANCE.

The Roman Catholics of Ireland *profess*, in the fullest extent, the doctrine of civil and religious liberty. This doctrine, if rightly understood, teaches that no man, who is a loyal subject and peaceable citizen, should be persecuted or molested, or deprived of any civil privilege or immunity on the score of peculiarities in religion; that is, whether his creed be considered orthodox or otherwise. The charge of intolerance against the Roman Catholic religion or Roman Catholic church, is of long standing, and rests upon very substantial proofs.

John Locke, who was a strenuous advocate for civil and religious liberty, would not, however, accord that privilege to Roman Catholics, because he considered them intolerant by principle. It was the supposed truth of this heinous charge that principally gave rise to the enactment of the penal code. The Protestants of these countries, who, though divided among themselves, on some minor points of religion, still latterly lived together like Christians, considered themselves justified in showing little favour to a church which would leave no alternative to dissenters but either conformity or persecution. In examining this question we should look to times past and times present.

It was a point not to be disputed in ancient times, that heretics were to be persecuted. To impugn church authority was worse than treason against the state. This sanguinary doctrine was supposed to be strictly scriptural. We find, in the indexes to the Bibles published by papal authority, subsequently to the Council of Trent, this bloody proproposition: "*Heretici tollendi e medio*: Heretics are to be exterminated,"* with subjoined references to the various passages in the Old and New Testament that are supposed to sanction or confirm it. In an edition of the Douay version, published in Dublin

* Sixti. V. Clementis VIII.

in the year 1791, we find the following note upon the 12th and foregoing verses of the 17th chapter of Deuteronomy: "Here we see what authority God was pleased to give to the church guides of the Old Testament in deciding without appeal, all controversies relating to the law, promising that they should not *err* therein, and *punishing with death* such as proudly refused to obey their decisions: and surely he has not done less for the church guides of the New Testament." The 12th verse, on which, in particular, this is a comment, runs thus: "But he that will be proud and refuse to obey the commandment of the priest, who ministereth at that time to the Lord thy God, and the decree of the judge, that *man shall die*, and thou shalt take away the evil from Israel." The doctrine of the note on this text, as above quoted, in regard to unfortunate heretics, is in exact accordance with the biblical indexes; that is, that they should be made away with altogether; always of course supposing the capability at command of doing so. There is here a coincidence between ancient and modern times on the subject. Tirinus, the famous Roman Catholic commentator on the Old and New Testament, maintains the persecuting doctrine of the biblical index, as that of orthodoxy, no doubt. In commenting on the third verse of the 13th chapter of Zacharias, he has these words: "*Ex quo discant Lutherani non solum in veteri sed etiam in nova lege hæreticos morte plectendos. Nam et proprii parentes, si zelo ardeant* *honoris divini, sententia et manu judicum, configent filium sic apostantem ;*"* which may be rendered thus : " Whence the Lutherans may learn that heretics are to be punished with death, as well in the new law as in the old. For even the very parents, if they glow with zeal for the divine honor, acting at once as judges and executioners, shall plunge a dagger into a son so apostatizing."

The same commentator again says, in his "*Index controversiarum fidei*," index of controversies regarding faith. "*Hereticos ab ecclesia damnatos morte et aliis pœnis multari patet ; quia sunt falsi prophetæ, qui, Deut. c.* xiii, *v.* 5, *c.* xviii, *v.* 20, *jubentur occidi: sunt rebelles summi, sacerdotis imperio, qui, Deut. c.* xvii, *v.* 12, *ex sententia judicis morte plecti jubentur. Et Christus non solum jubet tractari ut Ethnicos, Matt. c.* xviii, *v.* 17, *sed insuper dicit esse lupos rapaces ; Matt. c.* xvii, *v.* 15, *et fures ac latrones, Joan. c.* x, *v.* 8, *Similia habes, Act. c.* xx, *v.* 29, *Atqui tales omni jure occidendi sunt.*"

"It is clear, (says he,) that heretics, condemned by the church, should be subjected to death and other punishments, for they are false prophets, who, in Deuteronomy, 13th and 18th chapters, are commanded to be slain. They are rebels to priestly authority; who, in Deut. chapter 17, are ordered for condemnation and execution. And Christ not only commands them to be

* Vide Zacharias xiii. c. 30.

treated as heathens, Matt. chapter 18th, but also calls them ravenous wolves, Matt. 7th chapter ; and thieves and robbers, John, 10th chapter. You find, continues he, language of the same description in Acts, 20th chapter. Now, all such are to be put to death, according to every law." Thus far, Tirinus, a standard commentator with the Roman Catholic church.

Becanus, a famous theologian, who flourished about two centuries ago, enters into the particulars of this very serious question. "It is lawful," says he, "to inflict capital punishment for the crime of heresy." This language cannot be misunderstood. He proceeds—"In the old law, idolaters were condemned to death, and that by the express command of God himself, as appears from the 20th and 24th of Leviticus, the 25th of Numbers, and the 13th of Deuteronomy." These are his proofs, which whether they are good or bad, it is not our business to examine. Let us go on. "In the new law or under it the same punishment is decreed against heretics, as appears from the books '*quicunque*, cap. de Hereticis ;' and was always put in force for very cogent reasons. For why should not the new law as well as the old prescribe measures for the prevention of apostacy and the extinction of heresy?" He speaks here of provisions in the canon law, enacted by church authority. "This, (continues Becanus,) was the opinion of the primitive fathers and the law of the primitive church."

If he is correct in this, the thing is only to be the more lamented. "Even the great Augustine, (says he,) who, when newly converted was of the contrary opinion, in the progress of time changed his sentiments on the subject; and affirmed that obstinate heretics ought to be treated with the utmost severity.* And why, (continues our author,) should not heretics be punished with the utmost severity, whereas heresy is opposed, not only to the unity of the church, but to the tranquillity of the state? Heresy is more pernicious to society than theft, robbery, adultery, or murder; all which, for the common good, are placed beneath the lash of the civil magistrate. It is not, (he says,) in the nature of things that peace and concord can exist where temple is erected against temple, and altar against altar; for heresy is ever accompanied by pride, and pride is ever productive of discord. The experience of past times places the matter in the clearest light. What happy harmony prevailed among the children of Israel so long as they all worshipped at the same altar; but the golden calves of Bethel deranged every thing, dissolved the unity of the chosen people, placed ten tribes in opposition to the remaining two, erected a permanent wall of separation between them, and rendered them thenceforward strangers and enemies to one another. Have not, (continues he,) heretics from time to time excited

* Epis. 48, ad Vincentium.

tumults and kindled the flames of civil war in every part of Christendom? The Arians in the east, the Macedonians in Greece, the Donatists and Circumcillions in Africa? What confusion and bloodshed was caused by the Iconoclasts and by the Albigenses? What was the conduct of the Hussites in Bohemia, the Calvinists in Scotland, France, Belgium, and Poland; of the Lutherans in Germany, where the boors rose up in rebellion? In short, (says he,) the history of heresy is the history of discord, rebellion, massacre, and the subversion of all order.

"If the church in the first ages did not subject heretics to the punishment of death, it was because she was weak and impotent—unconnected with civil power and civil authority. In proof of which, it is sufficient to remark, that she no sooner became powerful and strong than she began to exercise severity towards all those who had the hardihood to gainsay her doctrines. She first inflicted the penalty of banishment;* afterwards pecuniary fines;† then confiscation of all their goods;‡ until at length, exasperated by their obstinacy and insolence, she proceeded to the last extremities, and subjected them to all the horrors of capital punishment, as we may read in the laws of Valentinian and Marcian, *lib. quicunque.* In fine, *religious liberty* being directly opposed to unity of faith and ruinous

* Lib. Ariani cap. de Heritic. † Lib. cuncti heretici ibidem.
‡ Lib. Mainche.

to the commonwealth, is by no means to be sanctioned; and it is lawful *and requisite* to protect orthodoxy by the infliction of pains and penalties, by the persecution of heretics, and the extinction of heresy." So far Becanus, who, as the organ or oracle of Roman orthodoxy, puts forth, with an air of triumph in all its naked and terrific deformity, the doctrine of civil and religious intolerance. Becanus did nothing but tread in the footsteps of his predecessors, Thomas of Aquin and the schoolmen, and gave, as he believed, the doctrine of his church. It is unnecessary to say a word of the doctrine of Peter Dens touching this matter. It is before the world, and coincides, as may be expected, with the biblical indexes of Sixtus Quintus and Clemens Octavus, with the note extracted from the Douay version, with the bloody doctrines of Tirinus, Becanus, and all the other acknowledged oracles and doctors of Roman Catholic orthodoxy.

All this must place our new apostles of religious liberty, Dr. Murray and the compiler of his directory, Rev. Patrick Woods, in an awkward and serious predicament. They must, indeed, either qualify the tenet of ecclesiastical infallibility, or declare themselves dissenters from the Roman Church. But let us proceed.

This doctrine of persecution is embodied in the Roman Pontifical. We find the following words in the oath administered to every bishop elect at the time of his consecration :—" *Hæreticos, schismaticos—pro posse persequar et impugnabo*"—"Heretics and schismatics, I shall to the utmost of my power persecute and war against." It could be easily shewn from church history how faithfully this episcopal obligation has been discharged in many unhappy instances. Was it not with the concurrence or at the instance of the pope and the church of Rome that the tribunal of the holy or unholy inquisition was erected in so many countries of Europe ; a tribunal that wars, *ad internecionem*—to the knife—with the principles of civil and religious liberty ? And have not churchmen, priests and friars, been always the great officers in these hateful establishments of religious despotism and intolerance ?

No man in former times dared to breathe a sentiment of religious liberty. The enlightened faculty of Paris, with Natalis Bedda at their head, condemned Erasmus for having presumed to recommend milder methods than fire and faggot to reclaim heretics. About the beginning of the last century, the Abbe Courayer was forced to quit France and take refuge in England, because he published a treatise in which he maintained the validity of the English ordinations ; and but a short time has occurred since the Catholic bishops of Belgium, taking offence at the spirit of religious toleration manifested by the Belgic government, made an official declaration, that the doctrine of civil and religious liberty is opposed to the principles of the Catholic church. This helps to shew that a coincidence exists between the past and the present.

Look at those countries that are commonly called Catholic, Italy, Portugal, Spain, Austria. Does the spirit of religious toleration dwell among them? Do they cultivate the sacred tree of civil and religious liberty? Or is it not undeniable, that wherever attempts have been made to undermine or overthrow the reign of religious intolerance, the whole weight of ecclesiastical influence and authority has been uniformly thrown in the opposite scale?

But let us come to old Ireland, where, if credit be due to words, and protestations, and oaths, the doctrine of civil and religious liberty is identified with Roman Catholic orthodoxy. Here Catholics have become so far Protestantized as to abjure the tenets and authority of Thomas Aquinas and his brother schoolmen, of Becanus, of Tirinus, of Dens, of the faculty of Paris, of the great Bossuet, (who was styled Malleus Hereticorum, the slaughterer of heretics, and who defended the revocation of the edict of Nantes); of the Bishop of Belgium, and of all the holy inquisitors on the Continent; besides that, for the sake of removing all doubt on the subject, the Catholic bishops in Ireland have affixed a new and satisfactory meaning to the formidable words "*persequar et impugnabo,*" contained in the oath they take at their consecration; which words, in their national church vocabulary, no longer imply "bloodshed and battery," as of old, but mild admonition and persuasion. Any question that may be raised upon this abuse of terms, we leave to the decision of philologers; for the discussion we have on hand does not regard words but things. *Non agitur de verbis sed de rebus.* The Irish Catholic church, therefore, disjoined and segregated, without precedent or example, standing upon its own individual merits, is all toleration and liberality. Very fine talk. Well, is this in reality the case? Let us see.

The doctrine of civil and religious liberty is altogether of a practical nature; and should appear in the overt acts, or in the conduct or behaviour of the class or body who make profession of it. Let the Catholic bishops and priests of Ireland be tried by this test. Have they laboured to smoothen the asperities occasioned by sectarian differences? Have they laboured to make persons of all religious denominations love one another? Have they extended the right hand of fellowship to their Protestant brethren and exerted themselves to extinguish the torch of religious bigotry? Have they allowed freedom of choice, in matters of religion, to those of their own body or communion; and raised no persecution against such as have thought it right to conform to the Protestant ritual? Have they shown any eagerness or inclination to cultivate the feelings of benevolence and charity towards the clergy of the established church and their flocks; or bestowed the meed of approbation upon those solitary individuals of their own body, or of their congregations, who ventured to manifest to the world this noble spirit of Christian liberality? Did they express their horror from the pulpit and from the altar at the open war of extermination that was carried on, not long since, by the deluded peasantry, and which would have still continued but for the Coercion Act, against the whole body of the Irish Protestant clergy? Or, to change the question, and to pass by minor charges, if the thing be fairly considered, were not they themselves, (the Irish Catholic priests and bishops,) amid all their fine professions of toleration and liberality, the abettors or instigators, if not the very authors, of this savage, bloody persecution; a persecution that still continues and has for object nothing more or less than the utter extinction of Protestantism in this country? What, after all this, becomes of solemn disclaimers and oaths of abjuration? What are we to say of Irish Catholicity, but that it is at variance with itself, and lies under the odious stigma of prevarication and perjury?

It is not in the nature of things that the Catholic bishops and priests of Ireland, under existing circumstances, or considering their constitution as a body, could be the true advocates of civil and religious liberty. Their own internal regimen exhibits a picture of despotism in its worst form. The bishops, who are subject to no control of church discipline or canon law, govern by caprice; and exercise occasionally the most wanton despotism. The priests are, in consequence, their fawning sycophants or slaves. They are prepared for all this by the slavish and inquisitorial training they undergo at Maynooth College.* Further, at the time of ordination, on bended knees, with hands enclosed betwixt the hands of episcopacy, as vassals or serfs, they promise the bishops obedience as their liege lords; and ever after, in approaching them, worship them by genuflection. The priests themselves, as naturally may be expected,—for slaves in imitation of their masters become tyrants in their own sphere,—endeavour to exercise a similar tyranny over their congregations. They are tyrants in the confessional, and tyrants at the altar. They make that which is innocent criminal; and that which is criminal innocent. They impose, under pain of damnation, fasts and abstinences, which they disregard themselves. If they take a dislike to a schoolmaster or a candidate for parliament, they hand over to his satanic majesty all who may send their children for instruction to the one, and all who may presume to exercise the elective franchise in favour of the other. What is all this but the worst species of despotism?—a despotism upheld by the aid of religious ignorance and religious imposture. Even the better order are in a great

* Vide the exposé given by O'Beirne.

measure deprived of their free will, and awed into neutrality. What great liberality of sentiment may be expected from a body or society so trained and constituted! First an arbitrary chief, much resembling the old Dey of Algiers—obeyed by a crowd of subordinate mortals, who, educated in slavery, are at once slaves and tyrants—meanly fawning upon their lord and master, but tyrannizing themselves over a suppliant multitude, who obey their commands for fear of everlasting damnation. The chilling cry of blind submission may proceed from such a quarter, but not by any means the cheering note of civil and religious liberty. What are the enlightened Roman Catholics to do under these circumstances? Either to liberalize their church or to abjure it.

CHAPTER XXXI.

OF CLERICAL CELIBACY.

Clerical celibacy furnishes matter for disputation between the two churches. This severe discipline has been universally decried by the Reformers, not only upon its own merits but also as having no foundation or warranty in the sacred writings. Its advocates, however, endeavour to deduce arguments in its favour from the nature and obligations of the priestly office, and from some observations of St. Paul on the subject of virginity. But the greatest sticklers for the practice are forced to admit, that it involves nothing more than a question of church discipline, and should, of course, furnish no grounds for a breach of communion between Christians.

The priests of the Greek church, like the reformed clergy, are under no obligation of celibacy. St. Paul, notwithstanding the high encomiums he bestows on virginity, does not impose celibacy on the preachers of the gospel. On the contrary, he says, " Let a bishop be the husband of one wife ;"* and he seems to consider the rearing up or governing a family, in an orderly, correct manner, to be a necessary test of the prudence required in a Christian priest, for he includes priest in the title bishop—" one that ruleth well his own house, having his *children* in subjection in all gravity."

Innumerable scandals flow from the enforcement of this austere discipline. The most severe laws are found on the statute book against sacerdotal incontinence; from the nature and provisions of which, to say nothing of facts that are constantly before the world, it may be inferred that it is a crime of frequent commission, and at times, under circumstances peculiarly scandalous. A special penal

* Tim. iii.

rescript or bull has been issued, by papal authority, against such priests as make the tribunal of confession subservient to the gratification of their unruly appetites. This crime is called "*solicitatio in tribunale*"—" the seduction, or an attempt at the seduction, of a female penitent in the confessional," and has, of course, been occasionally committed. The bishop reserves to himself the privilege of granting absolution to, or of granting special license *pro re nata* to absolve either the guilty priest or the violated female; which latter is placed under the odious obligation of betraying the name of her sacrilegious paramour or seducer to his mitred superior. This curious process, if properly examined, is tantamount to an infraction of the seal of confession. Clerical intrigues, in opposition to the rule of celibacy, are, it is well known, of constant occurrence. Such being the case, an ingenuous and disinterested person would say with the apostle, "Let every man (or, in other words, let every priest) have his own wife." But let us examine the question critically.

To trace the origin of celibacy, we must have recourse to remote antiquity. Heathenism had its vestal virgins; who, under the penalty of being burned alive, were obliged to preserve their chastity inviolate. The restraint, however, was not perpetual, but limited to the space of thirty years. They were taken into this order while yet children from six to ten years of age. For the first ten years they were only novices, learning the ceremonies of their institute, and perfecting themselves in every particular that regarded the future exercise of their functions. For the next ten years they were employed in discharging the duties of their ministry as priestesses; and the remaining ten years were devoted to the instruction of those who were destined to succeed them. After the completion of this term, that is, when they were from thirty-six to forty years of age, they were at liberty to leave the order, mix with the world, and choose any condition of life that best suited their inclinations. Here celibacy was not for life, and besides it was restricted to a few females.

Before the Christian era, so averse was the world from celibacy, that even polygamy was allowed and practised. The Jews deemed it dishonorable in a female to remain unmarried. There were no nunneries at that time; and as to priests and levites, who ministered in the tabernacle, and offered sacrifices for the people, they were not subjected to the yoke of celibacy. Samuel, who was a prophet, as well as high priest, was married and had children. Though filled with the Holy Spirit, he did not separate marriage from the highest functions of religion. Jephte's daughter, who fell a sacrifice to the rash vow of her father, did not so much regret the loss of life, as that she was doomed to die in her virginity. Her preparation for death, which lasted two months, was a continued lamentation for her unhappy fate in this respect. The Lord, in Genesis ii. 18, condemned celibacy, when he says, "It is not good for man to be alone." The writings of Solomon are filled with the praises of a good wife, and with pitiful pictures of the man who spends his life in a state of celibacy. He appeared to have no idea that the time would come when especial merit and sanctity would be attributed to that state.

In the New Testament, our Saviour, after having spoken of the indissolubility of marriage, except in cases of adultery, spoke a few mysterious words touching celibacy. "There are some eunuchs, (said he,) who are born from their mother's womb; and there are some eunuchs who are made eunuchs; and there be eunuchs who have made themselves eunuchs for the kingdom of heaven's sake."—Matt. xix. 12. Origen, one of the most learned of the fathers, took occasion, from this last expression, to make himself a eunuch. It is remarkable that no one of the early ecclesiastical writers was more addicted to the allegorical meaning of the Scripture than this same Origen, who, nevertheless, with strange inconsistency, understood this obscure passage in a literal sense, and reduced his interpretation to practice. This was a comment with a vengeance. But we are of opinion that Origen will have few imitators even among the most strenuous advocates for celibacy. The words quoted seem to imply continence through incapacity, and clearly refers to mere individual exceptions, as appears from the words, "He that is able to receive it, let him receive it."

St. Paul, in the seventh chapter of his first epistle to the Corinthians, commends such individuals as remain single for the purpose of giving themselves up entirely to religion. But, like our Saviour, he speaks of exceptions, imposes no precept, acknowledges that he merely speaks from himself, admits the preservation of virginity to be attended with great difficulties, and concludes that it is better to marry "than to burn." Neither Christ nor his Apostles imposed any precept of the kind; but the church, in process of time, improving upon the original establishment, or deviating from it, supplied the deficiency.

St. Jerome, who is said himself to have passed a life of singular purity, though during his sojourn at Rome with Pope Damasus, his intimacy with some Roman ladies did not escape censure, was, of all the fathers, the greatest advocate for virginity, which he extols to the skies in his epistles and in treatises written expressly on the subject. He was a perfect enthusiast in this matter; and accordingly to maintain his opinions, he fell into several extravagancies. He adopted the vulgar belief that the sybils were at once virgins and prophetesses; and he said that they received the gift of prophecy as the reward of their virginity. This was silly enough. He attacked Jovinian with great asperity, who had ventured to affirm, in a discourse published at Rome, that widows and married women were, *cæteris paribus*, not less to be commended than virgins; and that, in fact, the most eminent and most worthy personages of all antiquity had lived in the marriage state. He viewed Jovinian in the light of a heretic for speaking so favourably of marriage. But leaving St. Jerome in company with the sybils, and battling with Jovinian, let us come to St. John Chrysostome, whose morals were likewise of the austere kind. He frequently declaimed on the superior excellence of virginity; compared virgins to angels, and asserted, to put the question beyond all doubt, that virginity is as much superior to matrimony, as heaven is to earth. One should suppose from this assertion that he did not believe matrimony to be a sacrament. St. Ambrose, the celebrated bishop of Milan, pursues the same strain of anti-matrimonial declamation. He delivered from the pulpit and the altar, many discourses to this effect; and such an impression was he wont to make on his fair hearers, that the matrons of Milan judged it necessary at last to prevent their daughters from attending his discourses on that delicate subject. St. Augustine, who handled every religious subject, did not overlook that of virginity. Like St. Jerome, he fell foul with Jovinian, the champion of the marriage state; and maintained that virginity is preferable; admitting, however, with St. Paul, that precept regarding it there is none. St. Basil commends virginity, but says it is beset with danger.

These declamations of the fathers, which only regard nuns and cœnobites, had the desired effect.

The pagan world could scarce furnish nine vestal virgins; whereas the Christian community, at an early period, was overrun by innumerable groups of monks and holy virgins, who, rejecting the partnership of flesh and blood, fancied themselves the beloved spouses or beloved followers of Jesus Christ.

The law of celibacy, as it now exists in the Roman church, and which is opposed to the discipline of the east, is a mere church law, founded through mistake on the principle of expediency. The apostles established no such discipline, nor had they any authority to do so, as St. Paul himself acknowledges. Churchmen were then at liberty to marry or not to marry. The sixth of the apostolical canons runs thus, "*Episcopus aut præsbiter uxorem non abjiciat*"—"Let not a bishop or priest put away his wife." These canons, though called apostolical, were made subsequently to the time of the apostles. It is probable that at the time the canon quoted was published, some austere clergymen began to moot the question, whether they should retain or put away their wives. In the Council of Neocæsarea, held prior to the first Council of Nice, we find the following canon. "*Si cujus uxorem adulterium commisisse cum esset laicus, fuerit comprobatum, hic ad ministerium ecclesiasticum admitti non potest. Quod si, in clericatu jam constituto eo, adulteravit, dato repudio, dimittere eam debet*"—"If it appear that the wife of any clergyman had been guilty of adultery previous to his ordination, he cannot be permitted to exercise the functions of his ministry; but if she has committed this crime since his ordination, he ought to give her a bill of divorce and dismiss her altogether." It appears from the wording of this canon, that if the priest's wife had been well-conducted, and not given to public scandal on the score of adultery, he was neither bound to dismiss her, nor was their cohabitation a bar to the exercise of his ministry. Christianity had existed for about three centuries when this canon was promulgated. St. Basil, in his 27th canon, orders that a certain priest who was entangled in a marriage within the prohibited degrees, should be suspended from the exercise of his functions. It was not to the marriage considered in itself that he objected, but to the circumstances attending it. A canon was proposed for adoption in the first Council of Nice to oblige bishops, priests, and deacons to celibacy, but was opposed, and with effect, by Paphnutius, an Egyptian bishop, who said, that though he himself had spent his life in celibacy, yet he thought that this yoke should not be imposed on the clergy.

Nevertheless, the predilection for celibacy had been gaining ground, particularly in some dioceses of the western churches, where, at an early period, this austere discipline began to be enforced. Pope Siricius, who lived towards the close of the third century, enacted some severe canons against such bishops and priests as continued to cohabit with their wives. This must have been in the suburbicary districts. He speaks of the necessity of making examples of some, in order the more effectually to put a stop to "so abominable a practice." It appears from these words that this pope was in doctrine a purist and in act a despot; and it is also clear that there were bishops and priests at the time, even within the range of his own jurisdiction, who lived in opposition to this new discipline, neither regarding his opinions nor his authority.

Towards the close of the fifth century, in the pontificate of Leo the Great, celibacy had made such a progress in the west, that it was extended to the inferior order of sub-deaconship. It pleased this great pontiff that not only the officiating priest but also his ministering attendants should be free from the contamination of matrimony. Celibacy now every day gained ground by new rules and regulations made on the subject; which, at first partial, gradually extended themselves, and at length produced the effect of establishing it as the permanent discipline of the western church.

This extraordinary deviation from primitive practice was not, however, completed without much difficulty. From the perpetual renewal of the canons against married priests, and such as kept concubines, it would appear that celibacy was not much relished; and that the efforts of episcopal authority for its complete establishment, though unceasing, were, for a long period, unavailing. We know also that, in the middle ages, this austere discipline fell very generally into disuse ; and that the canons enforcing its observance began to be forgotten. This was particularly the case in the tenth and eleventh centuries. A general re-action had, in fact, taken place, but it was arrested in its progress by the famous Hildebrand, who, under the title of Gregory the Seventh, ascended the papal throne on the 22d April, 1073. This extraordinary individual—the most enterprising of all the popes, and the most despotic—directed all his attention, his energy, and his power, to the revival and enforcement of the canons respecting celibacy, and to the enactment of new ones, accompanied by additional pains and penalties. He made holy orders an annulling impediment to matrimony, and left no alternative to a trembling priesthood but either to discard their wives, or surrender their benefices.

Some, however, stoutly remonstrated against the unnatural yoke the Pope was imposing on them ; and even had the boldness to accuse him of having advanced an insupportable error—an error opposed to the words of our Saviour, who says, that all men cannot live continently; and to the saying of the Apostle, who prescribes marriage to persons of this description. They further observed, that this law, which obliged them to live like angels, by offering violence to nature, would be productive of great disorders ; and they sarcastically advised him to bethink himself how he could procure angels to take charge of their flocks, since he was determined no longer to commit them to the guidance of human beings. The archbishop of Mayence found it impossible for the moment to put the papal decree into execution. He was constrained for some time to yield to the complaints of his clergy, to put in abeyance his odious commission, and even to promise that he would make special application to Gregory to recall it altogether. So exasperated were the clergy of this arch-diocess at the determination shown at the outset by their ordinary to enforce the decrees of the Pope, that they threatened, in a body, if he persisted, either to expel him the diocess, or take away his life. Disturbances and riots took place in many parts of the continent on the same account, and the spirit of opposition to the papal mandate arose to such a height at Cambray, that a man was burned alive for presuming to say that a married priest should not be suffered to celebrate mass, and that it was criminal to hear the mass of such an unclean minister.

The letters of Gregory to the various churches, urging the execution of his decree, show that married clergymen were to be found in all quarters ; who, of course, entertained no idea that matrimony was incompatible with holy orders, and who considered the anti-matrimonial edict of his holiness, nothing less than a tyrannical innovation. But opposition proved fruitless ; every thing yielded to the unlimited authority and inflexible determination of Gregory the Seventh : a man, who no sooner became sovereign pontiff than he formed the vast design of becoming lord spiritual and temporal over the whole earth ; of being the arbitrator and sovereign judge in all affairs, civil as well as ecclesiastical ; of being the source and distributor of all manner of graces and favours ; of being the disposer, not only of all archbishoprics, bishoprics, and the other church dignities and benefices, but also of kingdoms and empires, and even the private revenues of individuals. This vast design he endeavoured, and not unsuccessfully, to accomplish by the dexterous and vigorous use or abuse of his ecclesiastical authority. Opposition quailed under the terror of his censures, interdicts, and excommunications ; he deprived kings of their kingdoms, princes and lords of their revenues and domains, and made them his vassals ; and as to archbishops and bishops, he rendered them so subservient to his high jurisdiction, that they dared not to do anything of moment in their dioceses, without his orders and directions. Such is the character of Gregory the Seventh, commonly called Hildebrand—of the man who was chiefly instrumental in laying the axe to the root of clerical marriages, and of planting the barren tree of clerical celibacy. Emperors, kings, and nature herself, sunk beneath the pressure of his authority.

The disunion between the Greeks and Latins, saved the former from the fate of the latter, or perhaps, ensured success to the enterprizes of the Pope. They continued, and still continue, to abide by the words of St. Paul to Timothy, " Let every bishop or priest be the husband of one wife ;" and they even went so far as to cast reproaches on the Latin church for having presumed to establish a contrary discipline. We may censure the Greeks for having quarrelled with the Latins about the use of unleavened bread in the sacrament, the fast of Saturday, which is now abrogated, the duration of Lent, the shaving of the priests, and the singing Allelujah: but we should hesitate to do so for their having disagreed with the Latins in regard to celibacy.

The abuses to which this discipline gives rise are numerous beyond calculation. Swift, in his Tale of a Tub, observed, that when Lord Peter commanded his two brethren, Martin and Jack, to turn away their wives, he permitted them to pick up with the first strolling baggages they might meet. Celibacy instead of promoting the reign of virtue only enlarged the empire of vice. It is constantly giving occasion to varied and indiscriminate profligacy. This has been the case from the beginning. From the fourth and fifth centuries downwards, scarce a petty council was held that did not prescribe new pains and penalties against all such nuns and clergymen as might fall into temptation and run counter to the purifying restrictions imposed on them. In the second Council of Arles, which was held in the fifth century, it was enjoined, "that no person in holy orders above that of deacon (that is priests or bishops) should have dwelling under his roof any woman, save his grandmother, his daughter, his niece, or his wife." This canon did not condemn married but concubinary ecclesiastics. In the Council of Anjou, held in 433, it was ordered "that priests should not dwell with women." The Council of Tours, held in 461, framed a similar canon; still, however, permitting priests to marry, "provided they did not make choice of widows." This clause was fantastical enough. The Council of Agatha, held in the year 506, in the tenth canon, "forbids priests to reside with, or frequent the company of strange women." And this same council also, considering, no doubt, the natural propensities of youth, ordered that the veil should not be given to nuns under the age of forty; that is to say, about that period of life when the vestal virgins of the pagan world were restored to the natural rights of social intercourse. The 28th canon orders, "that the cloisters of women, or the nunneries, should be situate at a distance from the monasteries of men, because of the temptations of the devil and the talk of the people." The Council of Gerunda, held Anno

577, "forbids *unmarried* clergymen to have any female housekeeper, save their mother or sister." The 20th canon of the council of Epaone, held the same year, "forbids clergymen to visit females in the afternoon;" and the 38th cannon "forbids clergymen and young monks to visit nunneries, unless they may have kinswomen there." The Council of Clermont, held in the year 535, in the 13th canon, "obliges priests and deacons to live in celibacy; and orders that, in case they be found still to keep company with their wives, they should be stripped of their ecclesiastical dignities." This was a great stride at once, and harsh enough in all conscience. The Council of Orleans, held in the year 549, in the fourth canon, orders, "that such clergymen as are bound to celibacy and do not observe it, should be deposed." In short, almost every council framed canons, either of prevention or penalty, respecting the sexual intercourse of clergymen—a decisive proof of the difficulties that attended the introduction of celibacy, its establishment, and the frequency of its violation.

The prohibition of clerical marriages did nothing but corrupt the morals of the clergy. It gave occasion to illegitimate and promiscuous intercourse, and to deep hypocrisy, from the necessity of concealment. The fatal effects became every day more manifest. The seeds of clerical immorality took deep and extensive root, until at length in the 10th century, trampling upon canons and statutes, church rules and church ordinances, upon every law human and divine, churchmen cast aside the flimsy veil of exterior regularity, and exhibited clerical profligacy in all its native deformity. At that inauspicious period, the clergy of all ranks shook off the restraints of ecclesiastical discipline, and reduced the statutes of celibacy to a dead letter. They did not all, indeed, enter into the marriage state, which would be only a return to primitive usage—a step not to be condemned ; but, opposing themselves to the divine law, they formed illegitimate connections, and the church, which was said to be infallible and undefiled, groaned under the influence of courtezans, and the domination of ecclesiastical bastards. Priests, bishops, and popes, revelled in all the excesses of sensual debauchery, to the disgrace of religion, and the scandal of Christendom. Ratherius, bishop of Verona, who lived in that age, says, that the clergy were in general so immodest, that scarcely a priest was to be found fit to be ordained bishop, and scarcely a bishop fit to confer ordination. He recounts several shocking stories respecting the behaviour of ecclesiastics, and he charges them principally with holding infamous conversation with profligate females. Pope Sergius and Pope John the Eleventh—the latter the son of the former, by his concubine Marosia—and other pontiffs of the same description, by their open profligacy, set the example to the inferior clergy of throwing off that mask, which might otherwise conceal their debaucheries from the eyes of the world.

We shall not go on to describe how the discipline of celibacy works at the present day, either on the continent, or in the remoter parts of the world, or in our own island of saints. "*Dies diei eructat verbum et nox nocti indicat scientiam.*—"Day unto day uttereth the word, and night unto night showeth knowledge." Daily and nightly there are wars and rumours of wars ; there are stories of nieces and housekeepers, and of servants and of neighbours ; there are reserved cases on the statute books, the *copula carnalis clerici sive attentata sive completa ;* there are all the actual cases, that are continually on the wing to the bishop, and all the other cases, which, despite of statutes and episcopal ordinances and episcopal espionage, never escape the lips of the parties concerned, but

> Lie buried in the deep profound,
> Ten thousand fathom under ground.

So let them lie, whilst we, not liking to say overmuch to the disparagement of our loving contemporaries, hasten to draw our general inference, which is, that the law of celibacy, being opposed to the sense of the ancient world, Jews and Gentiles, the chosen people and the uncircumcised, making no part or parcel of the new covenant, which, on the contrary, like the old, couples marriage with the priesthood ; being at variance with the apostolical canons, and the usages of the apostolical times, and with the discipline of the great eastern section of the church, and of the Protestant Reformed churches throughout the whole world; to say nothing of its opposition to the constitution of human nature, nor of the flood of filthy abuses with which it is continually inundating the social system; all these things being duly considered, we think that the obstacle which this questionable discipline presents to a re-union of the churches or to Catholic communion, should be removed without further ceremony, when all may chant in chorus,

> "Happy homes and altars free."

CHAPTER XXXII.

CONCLUSION.

We have now examined the chief points of dispute between Roman Catholics and Reformers, and endeavoured to show that, generally speaking, what the Reformers object to and have retrenched, either may, or should be separated from the Roman Catholic religion. The cumbrous machinery or ceremonial of the Roman Catholic church is manifestly the growth of time, and is a wide deviation from the original simplicity of the Christian religion; while the abundance of falsehood and superstition which enters into the huge compound is opposed to its very essence. For Christianity is based on truth, which, of course, should not be associated with lying and imposture. Upon this principle, an extinguisher should be placed on the false legends in the Breviary, which have caused such an augmentation of the ancient ritual; and upon the spurious revelations of Simon Stock and Co., which have occasioned the introduction and general adoption of so many superstitious observances, as absolutely to paganize Christianity. Let these retrenchments be made—retrenchments that are in accordance with the creed of every enlightened Catholic priest and layman, and what a stride would at once be made towards the approximation of the two religions. Let the Christian theology, which is contained in the Sacred Writings—the only unquestionable record we have of revelation—be, like tares from the good corn, separated from exploded metaphysics, which, groping in the dark, attempts to elucidate; and, working by inferences, to define as Christian doctrine what never was revealed. This profane intermixture has embroiled the church from the earliest times, and done an infinity of mischief to the cause of Christianity. Protestantism professes to remedy this evil. It ascends for instruction to the primitive ages, and it admits of no theology, save that of the Bible, or what is conformable thereto. Let this mode, which is plain and practicable, be adopted; and the consequence will be, that religion, stripped of its meretricious, disgraceful habiliments, will appear again in its native beauty and simplicity.

But, to particularize matters:—Catholics of Ireland,—(we address you principally, who are liberal, enlightened, educated, reflecting),—does the religion you profess, as it is taught and practised amongst you, stand in no need of correction and reformation? Will you join in the outcry raised against the man, who, for the sake of religious union and assimilation as well as the correction of religious abuses, has denounced scapulars, and habits, and such like things, as mere consecrated trumpery?—who has made war by word and by example upon religious bigotry and intolerance?—who has re-announced this pleasing truth to the world, that, between the enlightened of both religions there are not many shades of difference? No, you will not; you cannot join in the condemnation of such a man; neither will ye bestow the meed of approbation upon your own bishops and clergy, who, by depriving him of his benefice and driving him from their body, have shewn their determination to cherish the excrescences of religion, and to identify themselves with intolerance. He denounced as anti-Christian that novel abuse in religion which places the priest and the temple in the hands of a political faction, and completely sets at nought the sublime morality of the gospel. This was a sin not to be forgiven either by the priests, who profaned their sacred callings, or by the faction under whose banners they have enlisted. He gave a public exposé of well-known abuses in the collection of priestly revenues and in their occasional partition or appropriation; and which, as is evident, must prove a serious drawback on religion and morality. His object was, that a remedy may be devised for an evil of such magnitude. His statements were not incorrect. The picture was not too highly coloured. There was a lack rather than a redundancy. The statement, however, seemed to have filled up the measure of clerical and episcopal hostility against him; and, for a moment, to place in jeopardy the life of the man who was desirous of rescuing religion and its ministers from thraldom and degradation. They endeavour to stigmatize him with the brand of heresy. He retorts the charge, and accuses them of sanctioning the most revolting innovations, of practising hypocrisy, and of deluding the ignorant. If what they profess, and countenance, and practise, be the Catholic religion—which is not the case—he abjures it; he is not of their communion.

Countrymen—Read attentively the foregoing pages and judge whether the writer has made out his case. He has entered at large into questions which he only hinted at in his Essay on Ecclesiastical Finance. The attack made on him by bigotry and intolerance has drawn him out, and rendered it imperative on him to make manifest, by convincing proofs, that Protestants have not, without reason, set about the important work of retrenchment and reform. Dr. Doyle has admitted that the real differences between the two religions are trifling. He did not, indeed, enter into the necessary details; but his admission implies, that the Reformers have retained the essentials of religion. The author has supplied the deficiency of the Doctor; and endeavoured to prove to the Catholics of Ireland that if both religions be compared with apostolic Christianity, the Catholic and not the Reformed will lose by the comparison.

Read over what is said on the holy scapular, as it is called—which superstitious bauble you are to consider as a mere sample of a multitude of other matters of a similar kind engrafted on religion, which we have not time to handle in detail—and judge if your clergy, secular and regular, who are the high priests in this mystery of iniquity, with a full knowledge, too, of their own guilt, are safe guides to conduct you in the paths of religion and virtue; are not, in a word, the apostles of deception instead of the oracles of infallibility? If then, fellow-countrymen, the Protestant religion be simple and apostolic, if it propounds the great essentials of Christianity, if it contains the good seed of the word separated from the tares of error and superstition, (unhappily abounding at present in the religion you profess,) what alternative, what choice remains but either to retrench or to reject, to purify or to abjure? Let the consecrated trumpery, therefore, be cast aside, let the excrescences be lopped off, let the explanations alluded to by Dr. Doyle be amicably entered into, let metaphysical jargon be consigned to the tomb of all the Capulets, and the simple expressions of the gospel be the only language of theology; let the usages and doctrines of the apostolic times, or the primitive church, be taken as the common model for all parties; let all this be duly performed, and the happiest results may be expected. The clashing appellations of Papist and Protestant will no more be heard, the two religions will become one; and all sects and parties, losing their odious distinctiveness, will be commingled together and ranged indiscriminately, for the spiritual combat, round the common standard of Christianity.

APPENDIX.

No. I.

The Most Rev. Dr. Crolly, lately the Roman Catholic bishop of Down and Connor, but now translated to Armagh, encourages the circulation and perusal of the Scriptures. It is a cheering circumstance that this distinguished prelate happens, at the present inauspicious period, to be placed at the head of the Irish Roman Catholic church.

No. II.

LETTER TO THE REV. JAMES DALY.

Cnocanmore, May 18th, 1835.

Sir—A month elapsed from the time you received charge of the parish of the Ovens, until you were formally installed as parish priest. During that space, the benefice was still acknowledged to be mine. I am, consequently, entitled to a third of the receipts, which proportion I request you may send me.

I remain your obedient servant,

DAVID O'CROLY.

Rev. James Daly, Ovens.

REPLY.

TO THE REV. DAVID O'CROLY.

Sir—In reply to your note of yesterday, I have to acquaint you, that I divided the receipts of the parishes of Ovens and Aglis during the time you allude to *as directed by Dr. Murphy and his council.* I refer you to them for the grounds of their decision on that very *equivocal*, so far as your alleged claim is concerned, and, let me add, *miserable* branch of the question of ecclesiastical finance.

I remain, your's, &c.

JAMES DALY.

Rev. David O'Croly.

This well-written and polite letter needs no comment.

No. III.

LETTER FROM DR. MURPHY, THE ROMAN CATHOLIC BISHOP IN CORK, TO THE REV. DAVID O'CROLY.

[*Junius redivivus:* or a sample of fine writing.]

Cork, November 15th, 1834.

REVEREND SIR—As you have refused to appear before me, though cited, and peremptorily, on the 6th of this month, one citation being intended for three, in consequence of your having directed a second edition of your pamphlet, notwithstanding my disapprobation and condemnation, as appears by my letters to you, I am driven to the necessity of depriving you of the parish of Ovens and Aglis, which I hereby do, and of appointing the Rev. James B. Daly in your place, whom I have directed the Rev. Messrs. O'Keeffe and M'Sweny, the V. G. and Vic. For. of the district, to *induct on to-morrow*, after having received his profession of faith. You have signified your intention of appealing to higher powers, which you can do when you think fit.

I remain, Rev. Sir,

Your faithful servant,

✠ JOHN MURPHY.

This letter was not delivered until after the induction took place.

THE END.

www.ingramcontent.com/pod-product-compliance
Lightning Source LLC
Chambersburg PA
CBHW080511090426
42734CB00015B/3030